Solving Web Offset
Press Problems

Solving Web Offset Press Problems

Fifth Edition

**by
GATF Staff**

GATF*Press*
PITTSBURGH

Library of Congress Catalog Card Number: 97-74140
International Standard Book Number: 0-88362-192-4

Printed in the United States of America

Catalog No. 15185
Fifth Edition
Third Printing, August 2000

Printed on 60-lb. Cougar Opaque from Weyerhaeuser

GATF*Press*
Graphic Arts Technical Foundation
200 Deer Run Road
Sewickley, PA 15143-2600
Phone: 412/741-6860
Fax: 412/741-2311
Email: info@gatf.org
Internet: http://www.gatf.org

Orders to:
GATF Orders
P.O. Box 1020
Sewickley, PA 15143-1020
Phone (U.S. only): 800/662-3916
Phone (Canada only): 613/236-7208
Phone (all other countries): 412/741-5733
Fax: 412/741-0609
Email: gatforders@abdintl.com
Internet: http://www.gain.net

GATF*Press* books are widely used by companies, associations, and schools
for training, marketing, and resale. Quantity discounts are available
by contacting Peter Oresick at 800/910-GATF.

Contents

Foreword

The Graphic Arts Technical Foundation is pleased to introduce the fifth edition of *Solving Web Offset Press Problems,* a popular problem-solving book with its roots back to *Web Offset Press Troubles,* which was first published in 1966. Written by GATF printing experts, this book is an indispensable press-side aid for any web offset press operator.

Like the previous four editions, this book was the result of the input from a large number of GATF staff who are asked to identify and solve a wide range of printing problems on a daily basis. I would like to thank the following for their valuable input: Dennis J. Cook, senior technical consultant; Lloyd P. DeJidas, director of graphic services and facility manager; Brad E. Evans, materials testing coordinator; Frank J. Gualtieri, technical services director; John T. Lind, senior research chemist; Brian S. May, pressroom/bindery supervisor; Dillon R. Mooney, technical consultant; Raymond J. Prince, senior technical consultant; Kenneth E. Rizzo, senior consultant/technical quality systems; and Karl Williamson, measurement and analysis technician.

I would also like to acknowledge the efforts of Thomas M. Destree, GATF Press editor in chief, who edited and paginated the book and created most of the line illustrations; Charles J. Lucas, graphic designer, who created the cover design; and Erika L. Kendra, assistant technical editor, who scanned all of the photographic images.

Peter M. Oresick
Director, GATF Press

This book is dedicated to the memory of Dennis J. Cook,
a senior technical consultant with GATF,
who passed away earlier this year.

Dennis will be missed
by all of his coworkers and friends in the industry.

1   Introduction

Prior to World War II, almost all lithographic presses were sheetfed; the trend was toward larger multicolor presses. A few web offset presses were in operation; however, these were used mostly for single-color and simple two-color work. These web offset presses had no heated dryers through which to pass the freshly printed web.

Letterpress printers began using heatset inks in the 1930s; however, heatset inks for offset had not yet been developed. The success of heatset letterpress printing made the heatset principle a prime objective in web offset. As a result, heatset offset inks were developed, and heat dryers were installed beginning in 1948. Since then, improvements in presses, printing plates, blankets, dryers, paper, and ink have contributed greatly to the success and growth of web offset printing.

The adoption of web offset was slow at first but has accelerated tremendously since about 1950. Press manufacturers build web offset presses for a variety of applications, which include publication, commercial, newspaper, and business forms printing. Four- to eight-unit blanket-to-blanket heatset presses represent the greatest growth increase in web offset printing.

The predominant press sizes (widths) measure 36 in. (914 mm) and 38 in. (965 mm) with fixed cutoffs measuring 21¾ in. (555 mm) and 22¾ in. (578 mm).

Multicolor heatset web offset presses are being used to print magazines, trade journals, catalogs, books, promotional materials, and commercial jobs.

Most newspaper printers have converted from letterpress to web offset. Business forms are also predominantly printed by web offset.

The growth and popularity of web offset printing can largely be attributed to low cost and high operating speed.

A four-unit blanket-to-blanket web offset press with optional delivery to a folder or sheeter

The press configuration shown here is the most common, but variations are possible. For example, with some presses having more than six units, the folder(s) is placed in the middle of the total press configuration and the infeeds are placed at each end.

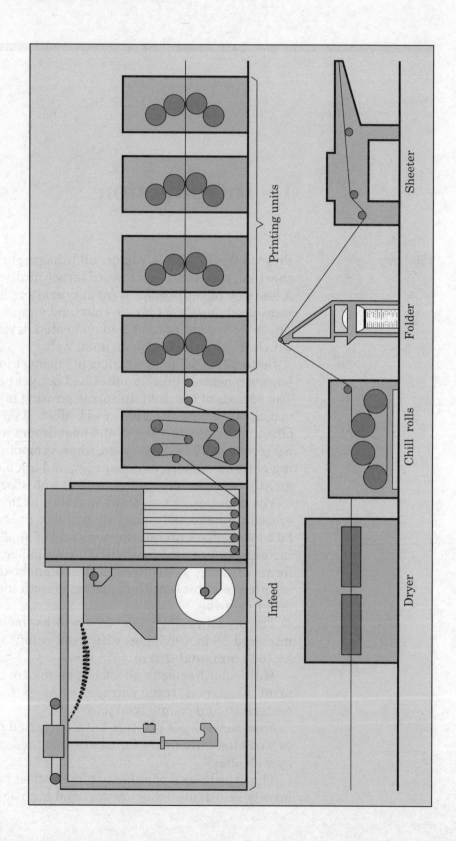

Printing units

Infeed

Chill rolls

Dryer

Folder

Sheeter

**Web Offset
Press Designs**

The printing method on a lithographic web offset press is similar to that on a lithographic sheetfed offset press in that both transfer images from plates to blankets to paper. Web offset printing couples consist of plate and blanket cylinders and inking and dampening systems. The plate and blanket cylinders have much smaller gaps into which the plate and blanket are respectively fastened; this minimizes the amount of paper that is wasted between successive impressions. On newer presses, the blanket cylinders may even be gapless, with the blanket essentially being a sleeve. The method of obtaining impression varies with press design (blanket-to-blanket, common-impression-cylinder, and in-line).

Blanket-to-blanket web offset presses. The most widely used design of commercial web offset press is the blanket-to-blanket press. The web passes between two blanket cylinders, each of which acts as the impression cylinder for the other. Blanket-to-blanket presses *perfect;* that is, they print on both sides of the web in one pass. The number of colors printed depends on the number of printing units. Four units are required for process-color printing; additional units may be used to varnish, to print spot colors, or to allow multiple webbing.

A typical blanket-to-blanket printing unit of horizontal design

Each blanket cylinder acts as an impression cylinder for the other couple in the printing unit. Blanket-to-blanket units have two couples arranged to simultaneously print both sides of the web.

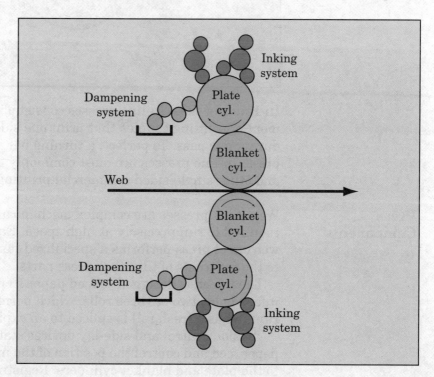

Common-impression-cylinder presses. The common-impression-cylinder (CIC) press consists of a large, steel impression cylinder that is common to all units printing one side of the web. Two presses must be run in tandem to perfect. The web is printed on one side in the first press, dried, turned, backed-up in the second press, and delivered all in one operation. A *double-ender* press prints a half-width web using one-half of each plate and blanket cylinder. The printed web is dried, fed back, turned, and backed-up on the other half of each plate and blanket cylinder. This is also a continuous operation.

The common-impression-cylinder press, often called a drum press

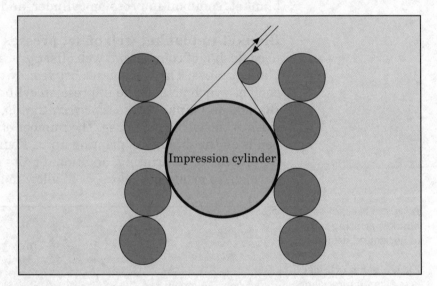

In-line presses. In-line presses consist of a linear arrangement of printing couples that print one side of the web during one pass. To perfect, a turning bar is added to the press. In-line presses are most commonly used to print forms and other single-sided commercial printing jobs.

Press Components

Web offset presses are complex mechanical systems that are required to run precisely at high speed. Each component of a web offset press performs a specialized function, interrelated to the functions of the other press parts.

The infeed is designed to feed paper from rolls. A typical infeed holds two or three rolls, which permits continuous running as a fresh roll is spliced to an expiring roll.

Tension control and side-lay devices stabilize the rate of paper feed and control the position of the moving web, relative to the plate and blanket cylinders. Registration — the proper

The in-line press, used for forms, cartons, and other one-sided printing jobs

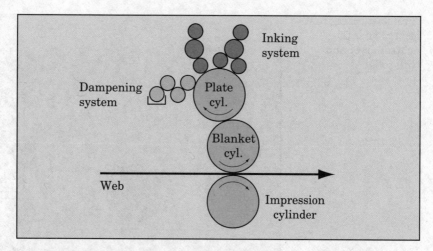

imposition of successively printed images — is obtained by controlling the tension and position of the web as it passes from one unit to the next.

For heatset printing, heated dryers are required to evaporate the solvents of heatset inks. Dryer temperatures may reach 500°F (260°C); the moving web travels through the dryer in about 0.7 sec. Therefore, the web is heated to about 300°F (149°C).

Chill rolls are used to set the ink, which is semifluid as the web comes from the dryer. Remoisturizers may be used to replace some of the water removed from the paper during drying. Nonheatset presses require neither dryers nor chill rolls. The inks dry by absorption into the paper.

The delivered web is usually folded and delivered as signatures, but it may also be sheeted or rewound. Specific equipment is required to perform each of these functions. Auxiliary equipment may be added in-line (connected to the press) or off-line (separate from the press) to perform additional functions.

Advantages of Web Offset Printing

High press speeds make web offset printing a productive method of printing long runs. A blanket-to-blanket web offset press running at top speed can print five to six times as many impressions as the fastest sheetfed equipment. Common-impression-cylinder presses produce up to eight times as many impressions as sheetfed presses. Blanket-to-blanket web presses can print on both sides of the web in a single pass.

Heatset inks adequately dry in a fraction of a second. Heatset inks lie mostly on the paper surface, giving high color strength and gloss with a thin ink film.

A remoisturizing unit located after the heatset dryer and chill rolls

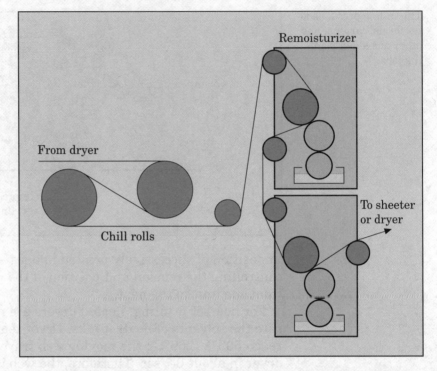

Auxiliary equipment attached to the press allows imprinting, numbering, perforating, diecutting, interleaving, coating, gluing, and other specialized operations normally performed in the bindery.

Lightweight papers that are difficult to print on sheetfed presses are easily handled. Embossing ("waffling) and curling are reduced. No sheet feeder, sheet guides, insertion devices, grippers, or transfer cylinders are required. Paper in rolls costs less than the same quantity of the same grade in sheeted form. Some low-cost paper grades can be run without picking or piling, further reducing paper costs.

Blanket-to-blanket presses can be *multiwebbed*. That is, a four-unit blanket-to-blanket press can print two colors on both sides of two webs, one color on both sides of four webs, or a combination of four colors, two colors, and one color, by webbing one printing couple as a direct lithographic unit. A limiting factor is the number of roll stands with which the press is equipped.

Disadvantages of Web Offset Printing

The cutoff (image length) is determined by the cylinder circumference; one dimension of the form is fixed. Layouts must meet this requirement. A press with a fixed cutoff cannot be used to print labels and packages. Variable-cutoff web presses,

A multiwebbed
blanket-to-blanket
press with four webs,
each printing one color
on both sides

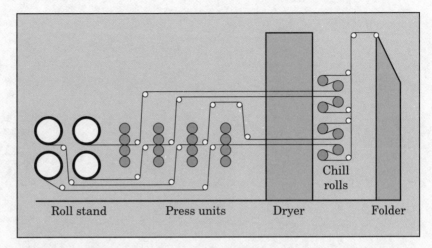

Roll stand   Press units   Dryer   Chill rolls   Folder

which are popular in narrow-web label and carton printing
today, overcome this limitation.

Makeready for web offset requires the use of new paper.
Previously printed waste sheets may be used during makeready when printing on a sheetfed offset press. Running
waste is usually 5%. Printers purchase paper by the pound;
wrappers and nonreturnable cores are included in the price
of a roll of paper.

The relatively small size of web offset press cylinders limits their accessibility for cleaning and adjusting.

For additional information regarding web offset presses
and printing, consult the following GATF publications:
- *What the Printer Should Know about Paper*
- *What the Printer Should Know about Ink*
- *Web Offset Press Operating*

2 Infeed Problems

The infeed stand of a web offset press is the structure that holds the roll or rolls of paper being fed into the printing units of the press. Auxiliary mechanisms vary, depending upon the paper, the nature of the job, and problems likely to be encountered.

Infeed Reel Brake

The infeed reel brake regulates the speed of the unwinding roll, so that the supply of paper matches the demand. The brake is activated by the position of the dancer roller, which varies with the amount of paper being fed.

Principle of reel brake action controlled by position of the dancer roller

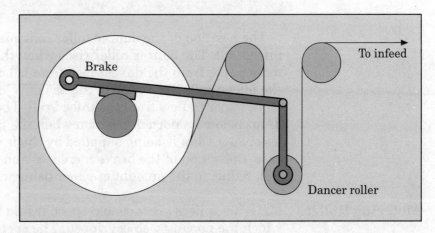

Dancer Roller

The dancer roller is a floating roller, the weight and position of which respectively set the tension and control the brake.

Tension in the infeed section of the press is a function of the effective weight of the dancer roller and is independent of its position. The following diagram shows that if the dancer roller weighs 200 lb., there will be 100 lb. of tension in each side of the paper loop that supports it. This is true regardless of the position of the dancer roller.

Control of brake by
rise and fall of the
dancer roller, with
tension constant

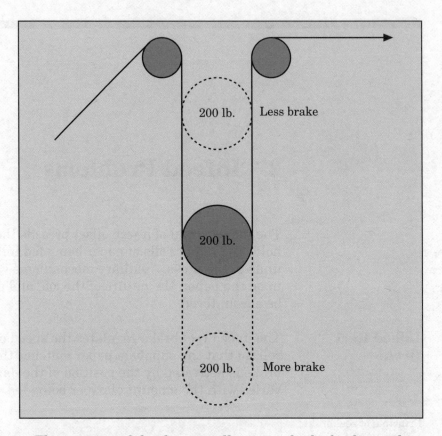

200 lb.   Less brake

200 lb.

200 lb.   More brake

The position of the dancer roller controls the brake on the
infeed roll. The dancer roller rises when the press is feeding
more paper from the dancer loop than is being supplied by
the infeed roll. The action of the brake is <u>lessened</u>, allowing
more paper to flow from the infeed roll. The dancer roller
drops below its normal position when the press is feeding
less paper than is being supplied by the infeed roll. In this
case, the action of the brake increases and slows the infeed
roll, reducing the amount of paper being fed.

Metering Rollers   Metering rollers are variable-speed infeed rollers between
which the moving web is gripped. The speed of the rollers
adjusts tension by increasing or decreasing with the supply
of paper; however, metering rollers do not effectively dimin-
ish tension variations that occur in the infeed.

**Constant-
Tension Infeed**   Constant-tension infeeds incorporate a second dancer, or
tension-sensing roller. The second dancer controls the infeed
metering rollers and is located between them and the first
unit of the press. The roller is not required to compensate for

variations in the amount of paper being used by the press; therefore, it is not used for storage. The range of movement (stroke) of this dancer is consequently small, reducing dancer-related tension variations. Because the infeed metering device offers inherently finer control than the roll stand brake, control by the second dancer is more precise. The second dancer minimizes tension variations, thus allowing higher infeed tension without the risk of a web break. Higher tension lessens blanket wrap and elastic recovery in the printing units, providing better register control.

Continuous-Web Infeed

There are two common methods of splicing a new roll of paper to an expiring roll without slowing or stopping the press. Automatic splicers are classified according to the running speed of the rolls when they are attached — *flying* and *zero speed*.

A flying splicer, or paster, splices rolls while the paper is running at operating speed (on the fly). Sensing devices monitor the status and position of the expiring roll. They detect when the roll diameter has decreased to a predetermined size. At this time, the paster rotates from the running position (which is also the loading position) to the splicing position. Meanwhile, the splicing arm and accelerating belts are also moving into position. The new roll is accelerated to press speed. At the time of the splice, a pressure roller presses the expiring roll against the surface of the new roll. Previously applied adhesive or two-sided adhesive tape holds the layers of paper together.

A zero-speed splicer makes the splice while both rolls are stationary; a similar adhesive is required. The press continues to print at operating speed, feeding from a reserve of paper. A collapsible *festoon* stores enough paper to supply the press during the splicing sequence. After the splice, the new roll is accelerated beyond press speed. This allows the festoon rollers to return to their original position and replenish their paper supply. Subsequently, the roll is slowed to press speed.

Sheet Cleaners

Sheet cleaners are frequently mounted on the press in front of or in place of preconditioners. These cleaners remove loose paper, lint, and dust from the surfaces and edges of the web before it reaches the first printing unit. Problems may arise if the sheet cleaner loosens partially bonded fibers from the surface of the paper but does not remove them.

Ultrasonic noncontact web cleaner *(top)* and narrow-slot high-velocity web cleaner *(bottom)*
Courtesy Web Systems, Inc.

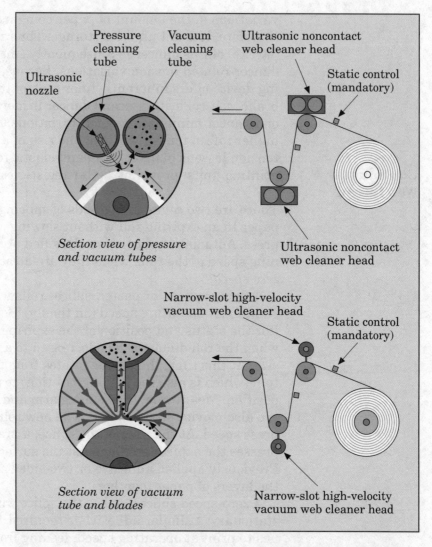

Pressure cleaning tube

Vacuum cleaning tube

Ultrasonic noncontact web cleaner head

Static control (mandatory)

Ultrasonic nozzle

Section view of pressure and vacuum tubes

Ultrasonic noncontact web cleaner head

Narrow-slot high-velocity vacuum web cleaner head

Static control (mandatory)

Section view of vacuum tube and blades

Narrow-slot high-velocity vacuum web cleaner head

Web Preconditioners

Web preconditioners or preheaters are located in the infeed, before the infeed metering rollers. Their principal job is to moisture-condition the web and burn off paper lint and slitter dust. Preconditioners may also help to reduce paper stretch and blistering problems.

Preconditioners consist of two sections that extend across the top and bottom of the web width. The web is heated to 175–200°F (80–90°C). Because of these high temperatures, chill rolls are needed following the preconditioners to cool the web so that its temperature does not affect the performance of the first printing unit. Hot metal in the preconditioner can damage a stationary web during a shutdown.

Web preheater
on the infeed

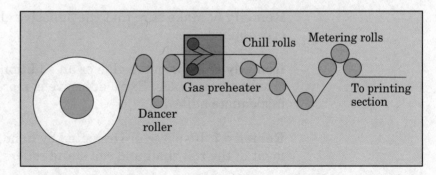

**Solving Infeed
Problems**

The following section lists the most common infeed problems, their probable causes, and remedies to overcome or avoid each problem. Some remedies may not be applicable under certain conditions. For example, the press may not be equipped with the devices that are recommended to remedy a specific problem.

Some chronic infeed problems can only be overcome by equipment, which may not be available on press. Management should consider acquiring the equipment required to enhance the productivity of the press. If the remedy suggests a major repair, management should schedule the repair.

Changing the paper or ink may not be feasible when the problem arises. Once paper or ink problems are diagnosed, the manufacturer or supplier should be contacted immediately thereafter.

Splice Breaks

Cause A:
The web breaks at the splice before reaching the first printing unit.

Remedy 1: On a flying paster, increase brush arm tension.

Remedy 2: Check to make sure the rollers are tram and level, and adjust if necessary.

Remedy 3: Determine the duration for which adhesive glue remains sticky without drying or soaking into the paper. Do not allow the prepared splice to stand longer than 75% of this time.

Remedy 4: When using glue, make sure that it is compatible with the paper.

Remedy 5: Make sure that the adhesive glue or tape is properly applied.

Remedy 6: Apply more glue or an additional strip of two-sided adhesive tape. Extra adhesive is more effective than inadequate adhesive.

Remedy 7: If splices are executed by hand, check the alignment of the roll shaft and roll stand rollers.

Cause B:
On a zero-speed splicer, the spliced edge of the new roll is rotated past the correct position on the pneumatic nipping roller; therefore, the leading edge of the tape does not completely adhere, subsequently folding back and sticking to festoon rollers or constant-tension infeed rollers.

Correctly applied splice tape on a zero-speed splicer

The lead edge of the tape aligns with the bottom of the nipping roller.

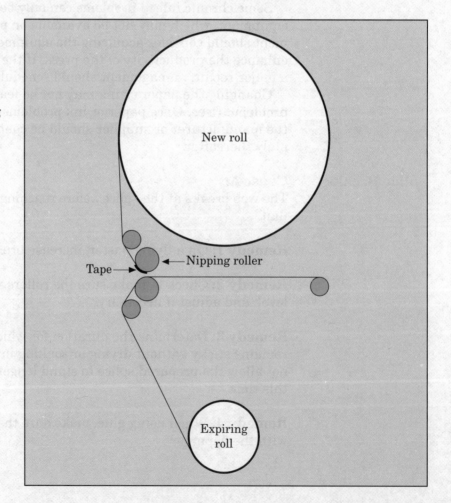

New roll

Tape → ← Nipping roller

Expiring roll

Remedy: Set the taped edge of the new roll so that the leading edge of the splice tape aligns with the bottom of the nipping roller.

Cause C:
The speed of the expiring roll generates excessive shock when spliced to the new, slower-moving roll.

Remedy 1: Make sure that the surface of the new roll (on a flying splicer) is rotating at web speed before splicing.

Remedy 2: Check the timing of the splicing cycle; adjust it if necessary.

Remedy 3: Reduce infeed tension if running lightweight paper.

Cause D:
Splice separates after the dryer.

Remedy 1: Check web exit temperature with a portable pyrometer. Lower the dryer temperature as needed.

Remedy 2: Make sure that the two-sided tape is designed to withstand the dryer temperature

Cause E:
Splice tape extends beyond one edge of the web and sticks to rollers or blankets. The new roll is not aligned with the existing running roll.

Remedy 1: Make sure that the rolls are aligned, or cut the splice tape ⅛ in. (3 mm) short on each side of the web.

Remedy 2: Check roll widths. Make sure that they are the same. Trim if necessary.

Cause F:
Rolls are of varying widths. If the adhesive is on the wider roll, it will stick to rollers or blankets.

Remedy: Apply the splice tape or adhesive across the new roll so that its width equals the width of the narrower roll.

Web Break
(no splice)

Cause A:
Press elements are misaligned. This problem can be identified by the appearance of diagonal wrinkles in a section of
the web between rollers.

Remedy: Adjust press elements that are improperly aligned.
Press elements in the area of the wrinkles should be trammed
and leveled.

Cause B:
Web tension is too great, or paper is too weak.

Remedy 1: Adjust reel brake linkage to relieve the tension.

Remedy 2: Reduce web tension.

Remedy 3: Reject weak paper.

Cause C:
Foreign matter accumulating on the ends of the lead rollers,
or loose grating on the ends of the grater rollers.

Remedy: Clean lead rollers, or repair grater rollers.

Cause D:
The paper roll is out of round; this condition causes a sudden
jerk with each revolution.

Remedy 1: Always store paper rolls of paper on their ends,
especially if they are stacked in storage.

Storing rolls of paper
on their sides can
cause them to become
out-of-round

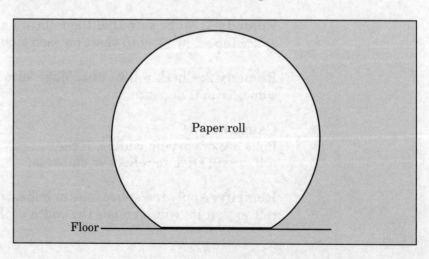

Paper roll

Floor

Remedy 2: Handle paper rolls carefully. Do not drop them or apply excessive clamp pressure.

Cause E:
Infeed reel brake overheats. This can cause seizing and result in excessive tension. Generally, overheating occurs because of increasing reel speed as the unwinding web approaches the core.

Remedy: Reduce automatic brake control near the end of the roll, and manually apply the brake as needed.

Cause F:
Ends of the roll are damaged. A crack or nick in the edge of the web becomes the starting point for a tear or break.

Paper roll with damaged edge

The outer portion of the roll that has been rendered useless due to mishandling. The damaged layers must be slabbed off the roll so that this paper does not enter the press.

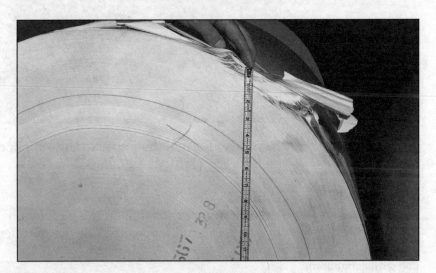

Remedy 1: Prevent roll damage by carefully handling paper after the end disks have been removed. A roll that is received in damaged condition should be rejected or slabbed off to a point below the damage — if damage is near the outer layers.

Remedy 2: Cut, sand, or grind out nicks. Take care to remove all small cuts.

Cause G:
Water in blanket gaps on start-up.

Remedy: Reduce the flow of dampening solution to the minimum required to keep nonimage areas of the plate clean. If necessary, let the plate catch up at start; clean up after the press reaches operating speed.

Cause H:
Edge cracks, wrinkles, or slime holes create weak spots in the web.

Slime hole

Remedy: Return the paper to the supplier. **NOTE:** Save both ends at the break as evidence.

Cause I:
Uneven draw or tension on the paper web. This can be caused by a tapered roll (opposite ends are of different diameters).

Roll with nonuniform diameter

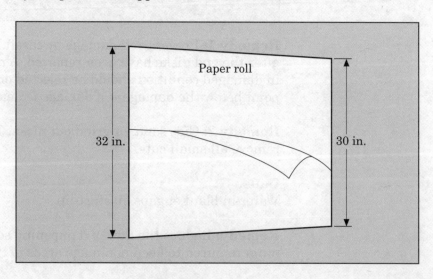

Remedy 1: Adjust the cocking roller.

Remedy 2: Do not accept tapered rolls from paper supplier.

Remedy 3: Check for parallel nip between the rubber roller and the constant-tension infeed metering drive.

Cause J:
The speed of the metering rollers is not synchronized with the cylinder speed of the first printing unit.

Remedy: Increase the speed of the infeed metering rollers. If the metering drive is worn and will not give fine control, repair or replace it.

Uneven Web Surface (feeding into first unit)

Cause A:
Web has nonuniform characteristics (e.g., basis weight, moisture content) from side to side.

Remedy 1: Reweb the infeed section to increase the distance from the roll to the first unit. Run with infeed tension as high as possible.

Remedy 2: Adjust the cocking roller to minimize the problem.

Remedy 3: Use tape or paper to build up the diameter of the infeed roller under the baggy area of the web.

Remedy 4: Reject paper.

Cause B:
Web is tight-edged due to exposure to dry atmospheric conditions, which caused shrinkage.

Remedy 1: Specify air-tight wrapping. Reject rolls that are delivered with damaged wrappers.

Remedy 2: Rewind the infeed section of the press to increase the distance from the roll to the first printing unit. Run with the infeed tension as high as possible.

Cause C:
Web edges are loose, because they have picked up moisture from the atmosphere.

Remedy 1: Specify air-tight wrapping. Reject rolls that are delivered with damaged wrappers.

Remedy 2: Reweb the infeed section to increase the distance between the roll and the first unit. Run with the infeed tension as high as possible.

Remedy 3: Use tape or paper to build up the section of an infeed roller under the slack edge of the paper.

Cause D:
The paper has wet streaks or moisture welts (which appear as lengthwise parallel ridges) caused by nonuniform moisture distribution.

Remedy 1: Reweb the infeed section of the press to increase the distance between the roll and the first unit. Run with infeed tension as high as possible.

Remedy 2: Spiral-wrap tape from the center to the edges of the infeed roller, so that the web is laterally stretched while running.

Spiral taping of a roller to flatten out the web

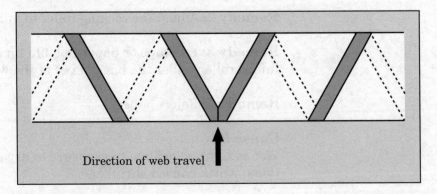

Direction of web travel

Web Weave (before printing units)

Cause A:
Web does not line up between festoon and stationary rollers.

Remedy 1: Make sure that all stationary rollers are level and that the festoon rollers are parallel to them.

Remedy 2: Replace worn roller bearing housings in the festoon section.

Remedy 3: Make sure that the web alignment controls are functioning properly.

Cause B:
Running a half web over crowned roller ends, either on the operator side or the gear side. The crowned roller ends draw the paper toward one side of the press.

Remedy: Adjust the position of the festoon rollers to compensate for the larger (crowned) roller end.

3 Printing Unit Problems

The printing unit on a blanket-to-blanket web offset press houses two opposed printing couples, each consisting of a blanket cylinder, a plate cylinder, a dampening system, and an inking system. The blanket cylinders serve as impression cylinders for each other. Thus, a four-color blanket-to-blanket press has eight printing couples (four on each side of the web).

Common-impression-cylinder (CIC) presses consist of a large steel impression cylinder that is common to two or more printing couples, each of which consists of one blanket cylinder and one plate cylinder with attendant inking and dampening systems.

On blanket-to-blanket presses, the plate and blanket cylinders are geared together, and the two blanket cylinders are geared together. The blanket cylinders of common-impression-cylinder presses are driven by a ring gear on the impression cylinder.

Proper functioning of the printing units depends on smooth driving and proper packing of the plates and blankets. Most plate and blanket cylinders have bearers to facilitate accurate alignment and provide the means for gauging the height of packed plates and blankets. On most presses, the bearers run in contact under pressure as specified by the manufacturer. Bearer pressure helps to smooth out variations in power transmission caused by worn or faulty gears. On presses with bearers that do not run in contact, the specified clearance between cylinders is set by means of feeler gauges.

The plate and blanket cylinders on web offset presses have narrow gaps into which the plate and blanket are respectively fastened. The minute size of the cylinder gaps permits nearly continuous uniform inking and dampening. The blanket cylinders on some of the newer web presses are gapless.

Cylinder gaps on
sheetfed and web
offset press cylinders

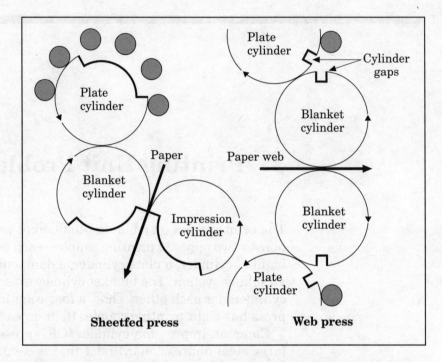

Plates and blankets should be packed according to the press manufacturer's specifications. Plates are usually packed 0.0–0.001 in. (0.0–0.025 mm) above bearer height. Noncompressible (conventional) blankets are usually packed 0.002–0.003 in. (0.05–0.075 mm) over bearers. Compressible blankets require more squeeze and are generally packed higher.

The press cylinders must be kept true and free from low spots. These could be caused by warpage or by objects (e.g., rags) running through the press. A web break and subsequent paper wrap-up could bend the cylinder spindles and produce eccentricity. Damaged cylinders cannot function properly and should be repaired.

Most commercial presses are equipped with hollow ink oscillators for water-cooling or heating the inking system to a specified temperature.

The following section lists the most common printing unit problems, their probable causes, and remedies to overcome or avoid each problem. Some remedies may not be applicable under certain conditions. For example, the press may not be equipped with the devices that are recommended to remedy a specific problem.

Some chronic printing unit problems can only be overcome by equipment, which may not be available on press. Management should consider acquiring the equipment required to enhance the productivity of the press. If the remedy suggests a major repair, management should schedule the repair.

Changing the paper or ink may not be feasible when the problem arises. Once paper or ink problems are diagnosed, the manufacturer or supplier should be contacted immediately thereafter.

Gear Streaks

Gear streaks appear in the printing, parallel to the cylinder axis. The distance between gear streaks is uniform and corresponds to the distance between the teeth of the cylinder's driving gear.

Cause A:
Improper packing of the plate and blanket. The blanket cylinder is trying to drive the plate cylinder, or vice versa, by surface contact. The surface drive exceeds the gear drive if there is not enough bearer pressure, if the gear teeth are worn, or if there is too much backlash.

Remedy 1: Measure the height of the plate and blanket to determine if they are packed according to the manufacturer's specifications.

Remedy 2: Increase the circumference of the *driven* cylinder. On most presses, the blanket cylinder gear-drives the plate cylinder; therefore, packing needs to be removed from under the blanket and added under the plate.

Cause B:
Lack of proper bearer pressure.

Remedy: Check bearer pressure to make sure that it is set according to the manufacturer's specifications.

Cause C:
Worn cylinder bearings.

Remedy: First, try the remedies for causes A and B. If none of the remedies works, check the preload pressure of the plate and blanket cylinder bearings. If the preload of the bearings cannot be improved by adjusting, then replace the worn bearings.

Nongear Streaks   Streaks in the printing run parallel to the cylinder axis; however, they bear no relation to the distance between the gear teeth.

Cause A:
Worn cylinder bearings.

Remedy: Replace worn bearings.

Cause B:
Inking or dampening rollers bounce when they pass the cylinder gap and strike the lead edge of the plate. This occurs when one or more form rollers is set too hard against the plate. The bouncing action varies the ink film thickness across the plate, producing a streak that transfers to the plate after one revolution of the roller. The problem worsens if two or more rollers of the same size are set too hard against the plate.

Remedy 1: Reset the form rollers to the proper pressure against the plate and oscillator. Make sure that the rollers are not driven by the plate.

Remedy 2: Check roller durometer.

Cause C:
Faulty bearings and either excessive or inadequate bearer pressure between cylinders. Under these conditions, two cylinders will move together when their gaps align, thus reducing pressure between them and the adjacent cylinders or rollers opposite the aligned gaps.

Remedy 1: Use the packing gauge to check the plate-to-blanket squeeze. Remove packing if necessary.

Remedy 2: Check bearer pressure; increase it if required.

Remedy 3: Check cylinder bearings, and replace them if necessary.

Cause D:
A loose blanket that rolls up and intermittently slips on the blanket cylinder causes streaks. Greater plate-to-blanket pressure increases the slippage.

Remedy 1: Retorque the blanket to the correct tension.

Remedy 2: Use the packing gauge to check the plate-to-blanket squeeze. Remove any excess packing.

Cause E:
Ink roller bearings sporadically freeze up, causing intermittent streaks.

Remedy 1: Always put new bearings on new rollers.

Remedy 2: Have the roller supplier press on the specified bearings prior to shipment.

Uneven Impression

Uneven impression can result from several conditions: uneven cylinder pressure, uneven or varying ink feed, stripped ink rollers, uneven dampening, poor or worn press plates, and defective blankets. This section lists problems related to cylinder pressure. Ink, dampening, and plate problems are covered in their respective chapters.

Cause A:
The offset blanket is nonuniformly thick, or is embossed by swelling and/or curing of ultraviolet ink in image areas.

Remedy: Replace the blanket.

Press operator measuring blanket thickness using a Cady gauge

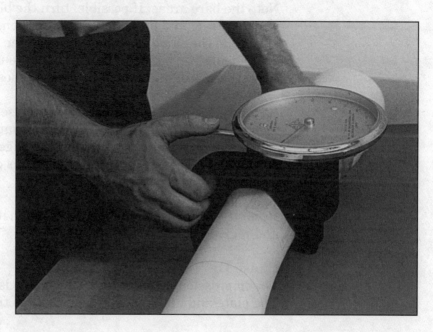

Cause B:
Plate cylinder is warped or dented. Check for this by removing the plate and packing. Then, run the press with a thin ink film on the form rollers. Lower a form roller (which is assumed to be true) until it contacts the highest parts of the plate cylinder surface. Take note of the depressed areas.

Remedy 1: Build up the depressed areas with tissue patches and shellac. Use fine sandpaper on a flat block to taper the edges and smooth down any high spots after the shellac has dried. This remedy is only a *temporary* solution.

Remedy 2: With the plates and blankets removed, use a dial indicator to determine whether the cylinders are within the manufacturer's specifications for roundness. If any cylinders are out of specifications, proceed to the following remedy.

Remedy 3: For permanent correction, metallize the cylinder and regrind it.

Cause C:
The blanket cylinder is dented or warped. Before checking for this condition, make sure that the plate cylinder is true and undented (Cause A). Mount a plate and pack it to bearer height. Pack the blanket to 0.001 in. (0.025 mm) above bearers. Ink the plate and pull an impression on the blanket. Note the bare areas. If possible, turn the blanket end for end, wash it clean, and pull another impression. If the bare areas appear on the same section of the cylinder, the blanket cylinder is dented or warped. Blanket bars are usually different sizes; therefore, this cannot be done on most presses.

Remedy 1: If the dent is not too deep, use shellac to apply tissue that has been torn to the appropriate shape. Use fine sandpaper on a flat block to taper the edges and smooth down any high spots after the shellac has dried. This remedy is only a *temporary* solution.

Remedy 2: For permanent correction, metallize the cylinder and regrind it.

Cause D:
The impression cylinder (of a CIC press) is dented or warped. The plate and blanket cylinders must be true to test for this

condition; furthermore, the blanket must be level. Roll up the blanket with a thin film of ink, and gradually bring it into light contact with the impression cylinder. Uneven ink transfer to the impression cylinder indicates depressions in the impression cylinder.

Remedy: Metallize the surface of the impression cylinder, and regrind it.

Cause E:
Plate and blanket cylinders are not parallel; the blanket cylinders of a blanket-to-blanket printing unit are not parallel; the blanket and impression cylinder of a CIC press are not parallel. Images will not transfer to either or both ends of the web.

Remedy: Follow the instructions in the press operating manual, or have a press mechanic parallel the cylinders.

Cause F:
Dirty cylinder bearers. Dirt on bearers separates cylinder ends and reduces pressure between the cylinders.

Remedy: Keep bearers clean at all times.

Cause G:
Excessive bearer pressure generates heat, which causes "bearer lift-off" when the bearers expand. The blanket appears to be printing low or uneven.

Remedy: Allow the bearers to cool. Recheck cylinder packing specifications. Reset bearer pressure to the manufacturer's specifications.

Slurring

Slurring is the filling in of halftone shadow areas and the appearance of fringe at the back edges of solids. This printing defect is most common when printing on coated paper. Slurring is caused by slippage in the impression nip between the plate and blanket or between the blanket and paper. Slurring can occur in either nip of a CIC press; on blanket-to-blanket presses, it occurs mostly in the plate-to-blanket nip. Slurring can be identified by the use of the GATF Star Target or the Dot Gain Scale and Slur Gauge.

Appearance of the GATF Dot Gain and Slur Gauge (Order no. 7011/7111) when slurring is occurring

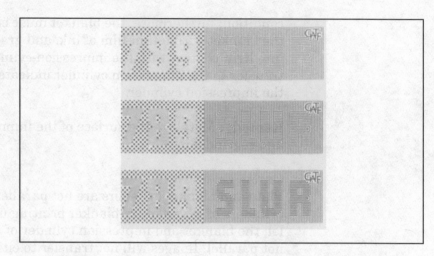

Cause A:
Too much blanket-to-paper pressure on CIC presses.

Remedy: Reduce the printing pressure to the minimum required to transfer the image.

Cause B:
Too much plate-to-blanket pressure, especially when running smooth (ungrained) plates.

Remedy: Reduce the plate-to-blanket pressure. Very smooth plates require approximately 0.002 in. (0.05 mm) of squeeze.

Cause C:
Too much ink on coated stock acts as a lubricant and aggravates slippage between the plate and blanket.

Remedy: Reduce the ink feed. If this reduces the color or black density, reduce the water feed. Adding alcohol or an alcohol substitute to the fountain solution reduces the amount of solution required to evenly dampen the plate. Consequently, less ink is required to give the desired coverage. Furthermore, a thinner ink film of a more highly pigmented ink may produce the desired density.

Cause D:
Ink is too thin.

Remedy 1: Use an ink with more body.

Remedy 2: Reduce printing pressures to the minimum.

Cause E:
Blanket tension is insufficient.

Remedy: Use a torque wrench to correct blanket tension effectively on most presses. The torque wrench needed depends on the blanket and the press. Make sure all units are corrected to the same blanket tension.

Cause F:
Piling of paper coating on the printing areas of the blanket. This usually occurs on the second or subsequent units of a multicolor press when printing on coated stock. It produces a mottle pattern caused by slurred dots.

Remedy: Switch to a more moisture-resistant coated stock.

Cause G:
Lateral movement of the form rollers slurs halftones on one side of the blanket-to-blanket press.

Remedy: Eliminate oscillation of all form rollers.

Cause H:
The printing units are out of tram, causing uneven vibration of units.

Remedy: Check the tram of the units. Take corrective action if necessary.

Doubling

Doubling is a register problem that occurs either between units or within a single unit. Doubling usually occurs when the ink on the blanket does not completely transfer to the paper; this leaves a printable image on the blanket. If the inked image transferred by the plate on the subsequent revolution of the cylinders does not exactly align with the image remaining on the blanket, a double image will transfer from the blanket to the paper.

Double images will print until all available ink from the first image on the blanket is transferred. Additional register shifts will also produce doubling. Doubling between units occurs when a blanket picks up a previously printed ink film. This is known as *backtrapping*.

Appearance of the
GATF Star Target
(Order no. 7004/7104)
when doubling is
occurring

Cause A:
The plate cylinder (driven by a gear on the blanket cylinder)
is forced to run faster by an *overpacked* blanket cylinder,
which has a greater surface speed. The greater blanket
speed, resisted by plate-to-blanket contact, creates forces
causing intermittent register shifts.

Remedy 1: Pack the plate and blanket according to the
press manufacturer's specifications.

Remedy 2: Check bearer pressure and reset if necessary.

Cause B:
Excessive play in the bearings or gears of the plate and blanket cylinders.

Remedy: Have the press overhauled and replace worn parts.
Doubling that occurs from side to side is usually caused by
end play in either the plate or blanket cylinder.

Cause C:
Low bearer pressure.

Remedy: Reset bearers.

Cause D:
Uneven vibration of units due to a floor foundation support that is unsatisfactory.

Remedy: Have units and foundation checked. Take corrective action if necessary.

Delamination

Paper is delaminated in the direction of web travel as it passes through the printing units. Delamination occurs only on blanket-to-blanket web offset presses, and is more likely to occur on presses with large cylinder diameters. Delaminated areas of the paper have rough edges and usually appear only on one side of the web. Delamination has the same appearance as blistering; however blistering is caused by dryer heat.

A paper web that has become delaminated but without a tearout

Cause:
A web tends to wrap around any blanket that prints a solid. When both blankets of a single unit simultaneously print a solid, the web wraps on both blankets. This may produce internal shear that is strong enough to rupture the paper.

Remedy 1: Reduce the tack of the ink. Delamination may be stopped by softening the ink on one side only. This prevents the web from snapping back and forth between blankets.

Remedy 2: Reduce the press speed. This will reduce the force required to transfer the ink from the blanket to the paper.

S-wrap, the tendency of a web to cling to one blanket and then the other on a blanket-to-blanket web offset press

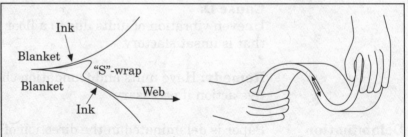

A web can wrap on both the top and bottom blankets at the same time. Delamination is associated with this type of S-wrap. In the right-hand drawing, the part of the paper between the two bends is under particularly high stress.

Remedy 3: Increase tension to reduce the degree of wrapping on both blankets.

Remedy 4: Change to a quick-release blanket that has a rough, ground surface, which reduces the force required to split the ink film.

Remedy 5: Reverse the web if the *felt side* of the paper is delaminating. The *wire side* is usually more resistant to delamination. **NOTE:** If solids are being printed on both sides of the web, this remedy may not work.

Remedy 6: Install one or more grater rollers to deflect the web and make it hug one of the blanket cylinders for an appreciable distance beyond the impression nip. This restricts the movement of the web and prevents it from snapping back and forth between the blankets.

  Some presses are designed with grater rollers to minimize web wrap. Other presses have staggered upper and lower blanket cylinders; this design automatically draws the web to the lower blanket cylinder, minimizing delamination.

Remedy 7: Check blanket packing thickness with a packing gauge. Reduce packing to the lowest specified thickness.

Rusting

Rusting of the plate or blanket cylinder destroys the trueness of the cylinder surface.

Cause:
Dampening solution seeps under the edges of the plate and soaks the packing sheets.

Remedy 1: Oil the backs of printing plates, attach the required packing, and apply more oil. This also prevents the packing from creeping during the pressrun.

Remedy 2: Clean the cylinder bodies every time plates and blankets are changed. Apply a thin film of oil, or some other rust inhibitor, to the cylinder bodies.

Remedy 3: Use packing paper that contains a rust inhibitor.

Remedy 4: Adhere a Mylar sheet to the plate cylinder. Replace every nine months.

Remedy 5: Use water stops on the ends of the dampening system.

Overheating

Overheating of the printing unit may cause excessive evaporation of heatset ink solvents. Reduced solvent content increases ink tack, which subsequently causes picking, splitting, and tearing of the paper. Increased ink tack can also increase blanket wrap, web flutter, and misregister.

Cause A:
Heat is generated by rollers in the ink train as they work the ink. Rollers and oscillators absorb some of the heat. Air-cooling and the evaporation of emulsified dampening solution have an insignificant cooling effect; therefore, the printing unit overheats.

Remedy 1: Water-cool the ink oscillators. Most presses are equipped with thermostatic control.

Remedy 2: Refrigerate the dampening solution.

Remedy 3: If a web preheater is used, install chill rolls to lower the web temperature before the paper enters the printing unit.

Cause B:
Excessive pressure between ink train rollers.

Remedy: Check the alignment and pressure between the rollers and oscillators. Reset to manufacturer's specifications.

Cause C:
The web preheater is excessively heating the paper, thus increasing the temperature of the printing units and inks.

Remedy 1: Reduce the temperature of the preheater.

Remedy 2: Install chill rolls between the preheater and the first unit. The web temperature should match the room temperature.

Chill rolls after the preheater on the press infeed

The chill roll are small and are driven by the web.

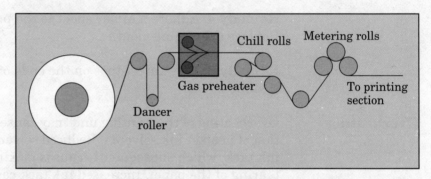

Cause D:
Ultraviolet (UV) drying lamps overheating the printing unit.

Remedy 1: Check installation to see that the proper heat carry-off is provided.

Remedy 2: Switch to water-cooled lamps.

Remedy 3: Increase the web lead between printing units.

4   Ink Feed Problems

The inking system for each offset printing unit usually consists of an ink fountain, fountain roller, transfer roller, ductor roller, three or four metal oscillating (vibrating) rollers, four or more intermediate rubber rollers, and two to four rubber form rollers.

Ink feed is controlled by the flexible or segmented fountain blade, the fountain roller, and the ductor roller. The distance between the fountain blade and the fountain roller, the rotation

Typical cylinder and roller arrangement on a blanket-to-blanket press

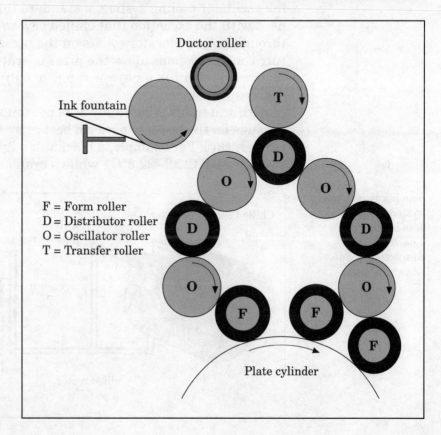

Ductor roller

Ink fountain

T

D

O

O

F = Form roller
D = Distributor roller
O = Oscillator roller
T = Transfer roller

D

D

O

O

F

F

F

Plate cylinder

rate of the fountain roller, and the dwell of the ductor roller are adjustable to feed more or less ink. The ductor roller alternately contacts the fountain roller and an ink transfer roller, transferring fresh ink to the roller train. The ink is worked to a thin, smooth film of printing consistency by the intermediate rollers and oscillators before reaching the form rollers. The form rollers apply the ink to the plate.

In order to function properly, oscillators must be power-driven at the same speed as the printing plate. The ductor, intermediate, and form rollers are driven by surface contact only. The fountain roller is driven either intermittently by an adjustable pawl and ratchet, or continuously through a gear from the press drive.

Uniform ink distribution around the rollers results from the differing diameters of the rollers and oscillators. Oscillators distribute ink over the length of the rollers.

Waterless lithography requires a printing press that is equipped with a temperature control system. Two types of press temperature control systems are used: an ink oscillator cooling system and a plate cylinder cooling system. With the ink oscillator cooling system, a standard inking system is used with the exception that chilled or *heated* water flows through hollow vibrator rollers on the press. These temperature control systems allow the press operator to maintain ink temperature within a narrow range of only a couple of degrees Fahrenheit.

With waterless lithography, it is not unusual for each of the inks on the press to perform best at a slightly different temperature. For example, a black ink might operate best at, say, 72–74°F (22.2–23.3°C), while a cyan might operate best

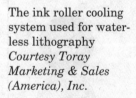

The ink roller cooling system used for waterless lithography
Courtesy Toray Marketing & Sales (America), Inc.

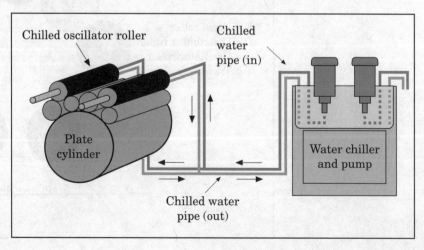

Chilled oscillator roller

Chilled water pipe (in)

Plate cylinder

Water chiller and pump

Chilled water pipe (out)

The plate cylinder cooling system used for waterless lithography *Courtesy Toray Marketing & Sales (America), Inc.*

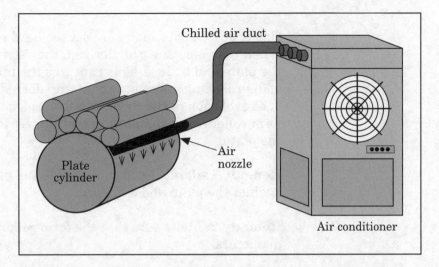

at, say, 68–70°F (20–21.1°C). (**NOTE:** These temperatures are examples only, not necessarily the temperature range that you will experience on your press.) Therefore, the temperature of each inking system on the press is independently controlled by using a zone control unit that blends hot and cold water to the proper temperature for the ink being used. In addition, infrared sensors monitor the temperature of each printing unit, providing immediate feedback to maintain the proper temperature level.

The following section lists the most common ink feed problems, their probable causes, and remedies to overcome or avoid each problem. Some remedies may not be applicable under certain conditions. For example, the press may not be equipped with the devices that are recommended to remedy a specific problem.

Some chronic ink feed problems can only be overcome by equipment, which may not be available on press. Management should consider acquiring the equipment required to enhance the productivity of the press. If the remedy suggests a major repair, management should schedule the repair.

Changing the paper or ink may not be feasible. Once paper or ink problems are diagnosed, the manufacturer or supplier should be contacted immediately thereafter.

Roller and Blanket Streaks

Roller and blanket streaks always parallel the axes of the rollers and cylinders. Single or multiple streaks may appear in the printing at equal or irregular intervals, with no relation to cylinder drive gears.

Cause A:

One or more form rollers are set too hard against the plate. When they pass the cylinder gap, they strike the lead edge of the plate and bounce. This ruptures the ink film from end to end, producing a streak that is transferred to the plate after one revolution of the roller. More streaks appear if several form rollers of the same diameter are set too hard against the plate.

Remedy 1: Reset the form rollers to the proper pressure against the plate and oscillator.

Remedy 2: Make sure that the form rollers are of different diameters.

Cause B:

Form rollers that are set with unequal pressure against a oscillator and the plate skid and produce streaks. Harder settings create a greater driving force and the form roller is driven more slowly. Thus, the form roller skids on the surface where the setting is lighter and produces streaks. Skidding is more likely to occur between glazed rollers.

Remedy 1: Reset the form rollers with equal pressures against the oscillators and plate. First, release all the roller pressures, so they spin free. Then, reset one form roller at a time, starting with the first ink form roller.

Remedy 2: Recondition the form rollers and oscillators to remove the glaze. Glaze is due to accumulations of dried ink and gum residue.

Photomicrographs of the surface of a new roller *(left)* and a glazed roller *(right)* *Courtesy Böttcher America Corp.*

 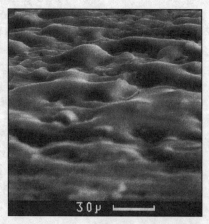

Cause C:
Too much pressure and/or too little bearer pressure between cylinders. Such incorrect pressure can cause cylinder movement when the cylinder gaps align. If excessive pressure exists between the plate and blanket cylinders, streaks will be produced where the form rollers touch the plate. Streaks can also be generated in the plate/blanket nip.

Remedy: Correct packing and/or bearer pressure(s).

Cause D:
A loose and slipping blanket. Packing differences between the plate and blanket cylinders create unequal surface

How a loose blanket can slip on its cylinder and cause slurring and streaks

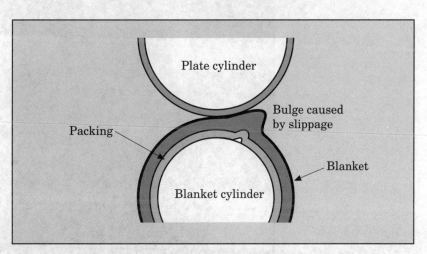

speeds. If the blanket is loose, it may adhere to the plate and slip on the blanket cylinder. The slippage is intermittent, causing streaks. Greater plate-to-blanket pressure causes more slippage.

Remedy: Tighten the blanket to the recommended torque. Use the packing gauge to check the height of the plate and blanket. Remove any excess packing.

Cause E:
Roller durometer is too hard.

Remedy: When roller durometer increases 15–20 points beyond the manufacturer's specifications, replace the roller.

**Uneven
Ink Feed**

Cause A:
Stripped ink oscillators and/or rollers. This results from glazed oscillators or rollers, or from using too much gum, etch, or both in the dampening solution. The rollers become preferentially wet and do not pick up and transfer ink. Metal oscillators are more likely to strip than form rollers, which also strip if they become glazed.

A metal roller that is stripping

Remedy 1: Wash up the press.

Remedy 2: If only the metal oscillators are stripping, wash the ink from the system, remove the form and intermediate rollers, and scrub the metal oscillators.

Remedy 3: If the rubber rollers strip, remove the glaze by scrubbing.

Remedy 4: Regrind the rubber rollers.

Remedy 5: Cover the steel oscillators with ebonite, or electroplate them with copper.

Remedy 6: Use hot water (180°F, 80°C) with vinegar at each major washup; this removes calcium carbonate.

Cause B:
Low spots in oscillators, intermediate rubber rollers, or form rollers prevent uniform contact and ink transfer.

Remedy: Remove and regrind the defective rollers.

Cause C:
Roller cores or spindles are bent.

Remedy: Remove the defective rollers and their coverings. Straighten the cores or spindles, and re-cover the rollers.

Cause D:
The fountain blade has become bent or has worn unevenly and developed a wavy edge. These conditions prevent accurate ink feed adjustment.

Remedy: Install a new fountain blade. Make sure that the thumbscrews are backed off and that they turn freely. Use the thumbscrews and a feeler gauge to adjust the blade according to the press manufacturer's instructions. Further adjust the blade according to the job requirements.
    Never force the blade against the fountain roller; this causes uneven wear and may score the fountain roller. Tighten the blade starting with the center screws and alternating toward each end. Loosen the blade starting with the end screws and alternating toward the center. This prevents the blade from buckling or kinking. Never completely tighten one screw while the others are loose; this could also bend the blade.

Cause E:
Dried ink or dirt accumulates between the fountain blade and roller.

Remedy: Keep the blade and fountain roller clean at all times.

Cause F:
The rubber at the ends of one or more rollers swells, peels, or blisters because the washup attachment does not completely

clean the ends of the rollers. This causes poor inking along the sides of the plate.

Remedy: When the machine washup is completed, wipe the ends of the rollers and oscillators. Replace damaged rollers.

CAUTION: Stop the press and engage the SAFE before cleaning accessible sections of the rollers and oscillators. Inch the press to expose the next segments to be cleaned. Do not clean rollers while they are moving.

Decreasing Print Density

The printed image gradually loses density or becomes grainy during the pressrun.

Cause A:
Loss of printing pressure. A new blanket is packed to the proper height for adequate squeeze; however, it becomes thinner due to mounting tension and running compaction. Plate-to-blanket and blanket-to-paper pressures decrease.

A packing gauge designed for achieving consistent and controlled results in cylinder packing

Remedy: Use a packing gauge to check the heights of the plate and blanket, relative to the bearers of their respective cylinders. If there is not enough squeeze between the plate and blanket cylinders, add the required amount of packing under the blanket.

Cause B:
Ink appears to back away from the fountain roller; actually, the ink sets up in the fountain and stops flowing down to the fountain roller.

Remedy 1: Install a mechanical ink fountain agitator.

Remedy 2: Frequently work the ink in the fountain to keep it fluid.

Mechanical ink agitator

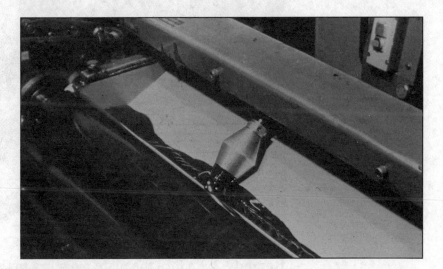

Cause C:
Ink builds, piles, or cakes on rollers and on image areas of the plate and blanket. The ink fails to transfer properly, resulting in graininess or reduced density. Incompletely dispersed pigments or waterlogged inks cause piling.

Blanket piling

Remedy 1: Check the degree of pigment dispersion in the ink, using a fineness-of-grind gauge or Grindometer. If the test shows many coarse particles or aggregates, have the ink reground.

A fineness-of-grind gauge, which is used to check the pigment dispersion in an ink

Remedy 2: Reduce the plate moisture to the minimum required to keep the nonimage areas clean.

Remedy 3: Add a small amount of suitable varnish to the ink, or use an ink that resists waterlogging.

Cause D:
Ink rollers become contaminated with lint and/or pickouts from the paper. Ink on the image areas of the plate and blanket are similarly affected. The paper particles absorb water, become ink-repellent, and thus prevent the transfer of a continuous ink film.

Remedy 1: Wash all ink from the press rollers with the washup attachment. Then, hand-wash the rollers and oscillators to remove the lint and pick-outs.

Remedy 2: Use a paper that produces less lint and resists picking.

Remedy 3: Soften the ink as much as possible to reduce its ability to pick up lint and paper particles.

Remedy 4: Apply roller cleaning compound to rollers and let stand at least 24 hours, and then remove using roller wash and water. Repeat this procedure twice a month.

Remedy 5: Use the best quick-release blanket available.

Cause E:

Excessive bearer pressure generates heat, which causes the bearers to expand. As a result, the cylinders separate, and pressure in the nip decreases.

Remedy: Allow cylinder bearers to cool, and reset bearer pressure according to manufacturer's specifications.

NOTE: Ultraviolet inks can attack bearing grease if they become mixed by way of the ductor roller, causing seizure and severe press damage. Keep bearing grease cups full.

Mechanical Ghosting

Ghost images appear in solids.

Cause:

A narrow solid ahead of or behind a wider solid consumes much of the ink on the form rollers; therefore, there is not

Mechanical ghosting caused by the design of the printing form

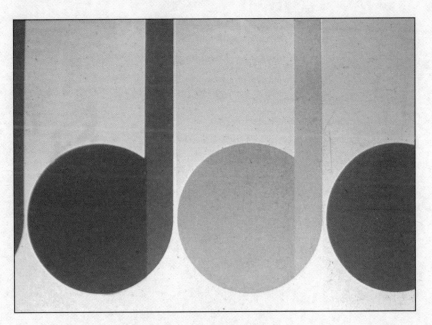

enough ink to print a full-strength solid in the adjacent areas of the wider solid. Lateral distribution does not provide the extra ink in narrow sections needed to prevent ghosting.

Remedy 1: Whenever possible, multiple solids in a single form should be well-distributed.

Remedy 2: Run the minimum amount of dampening solution required to keep nonimage areas of the plate clean.

Remedy 3: Do not decrease ink film thickness to produce tints. Obtain a weaker color that can be run with a thicker ink film.

Remedy 4: If possible, use opaque inks rather than transparent inks.

Remedy 5: Decrease the movement of the oscillators. This confines more ink to narrow areas of high demand, which may reduce ghosting.

Remedy 6: Install one or two oscillating form rollers to eliminate ghosting.

NOTE: Oscillating ink form rollers may slur halftones.

5 Dampening Problems

Web press dampening systems are essentially the same as those on sheetfed presses. The conventional system consists of a water pan (fountain), fountain roller, ductor roller, distributor roller (oscillator), and one or two dampening form rollers.

The slowly rotating fountain roller is partially submerged in the dampening, or fountain, solution. The roller is usually made of stainless steel, chrome-plated steel, or ceramic and is controlled by a variable-speed drive.

Conventional
dampening system

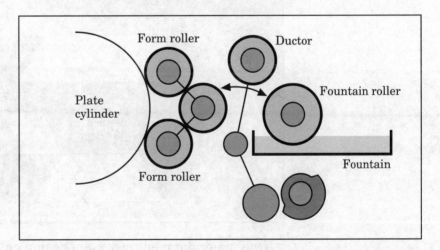

The conventional ductor roller is a fabric- or paper-covered roller that alternately contacts the fountain roller and the distributing roller. Its dwell against the fountain roller is adjustable and regulates the amount of moisture fed to the dampeners. The variable speed of the fountain roller permits the press operator to finely adjust the amount of water feed.

The distributor roller is usually made of stainless steel, chrome-plated steel, or ceramic. It constantly contacts the dampening rollers and is driven at the same surface speed of the properly packed plate.

Historically, dampening systems have included one or more molleton-covered rollers. Dampening systems that employ these rollers may require several minutes to adjust to a change in the dampening setting. To reduce the response time of the dampening system, use roller covers with less water storage capacity. Some storage capability is required to adequately dampen the plate at all times and to minimize the effects of surging dampening solution in an intermittently fed system. The problem of surging is greatest in a system that is run with bareback form rollers. Diverse roller covers exhibit various storage capacities.

Three methods of applying parchment paper covers on dampening rollers

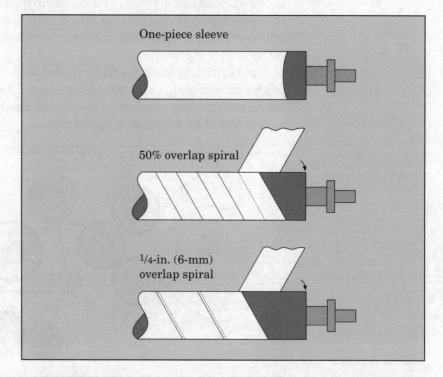

One major dampening system design employs a brush system. A brush roller is mounted above the fountain pan roller. The bristles of the brush roller ride in contact with the variable-speed fountain pan roller. The brush roller rotates at a constant speed and is set at a constant pressure against the fountain pan roller. This pressure is great enough to flex the bristles. The bristles flick solution at the oscillator, which is not in contact with the brush. The amount of solution fed is varied by changing the speed of the fountain pan roller,

The Heidelberg Harris
brush dampening
system

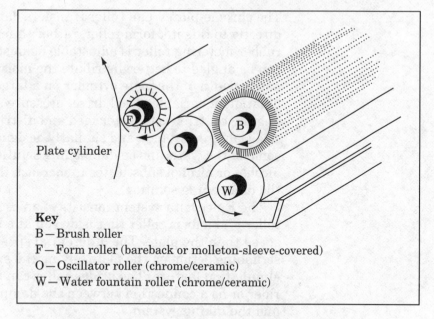

Plate cylinder

Key
B — Brush roller
F — Form roller (bareback or molleton-sleeve-covered)
O — Oscillator roller (chrome/ceramic)
W — Water fountain roller (chrome/ceramic)

and water flow can be modulated across the press by using water stops. This system uses a single form roller that is often run bareback (without a cover).

One continuous-flow dampening system is the Dahlgren dampening system, which consists of a rubber-covered metering roller that runs in contact with a highly polished chrome-plated pan roller. These rollers are geared together and driven by a dedicated variable-speed motor. The pan roller runs in constant contact with the first ink form roller.

The Dahlgren
dampening system,
an example of an
inker-feed system

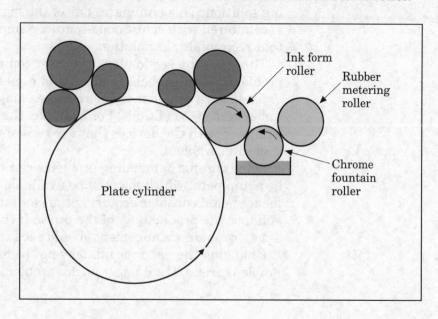

Ink form
roller

Rubber
metering
roller

Chrome
fountain
roller

Plate cylinder

The chrome-plated pan roller transfers dampening solution directly to this ink form roller, rather than to the plate. The rubber metering roller is adjustable against the pan roller and can be angled to better distribute the moisture across the entire width of the plate cylinder on a large press. The combination of variable-speed drive, pressure adjustment, and angling contribute to water-feed and distribution control. The Dahlgren system, and similarly designed systems, replace some of the water in the dampening solution with isopropyl alcohol or alcohol substitutes to increase the wettability of the dampening solution.

The Epic Delta system consists of an oscillating bridge roller and a form roller that is driven at a slower surface speed than the plate. The differential speed results in a scrubbing action on the plate, giving the system a hickey-elimination feature. The bridge roller can be used either as a rider or as a connection between the dampening form roller and the inking system.

Several dampening systems spray fine mists of solution directly onto the rollers of their respective inking systems. The spray comes from a row of nozzles mounted on a bar across the press. Each nozzle can be independently metered. As indicated in the drawing on the facing page, there is no recirculation of dampening solution. This is a distinct advantage in that fresh dampening solution constantly dampens the plate. The reduced exposure to atmospheric and press conditions virtually eliminates any changes in the dampening solution. This eliminates one of the big drawbacks encountered with continuous-contact dampening systems that recirculate the solution.

The following section lists the most common dampening problems, their probable causes, and remedies to overcome or avoid each problem. Some remedies may not be applicable under certain conditions. For example, the press may not be equipped with the devices that are recommended to remedy a specific problem.

Some chronic dampening problems can only be overcome by equipment, which may not be available on press. Management should consider acquiring the equipment required to enhance the productivity of the press. If the remedy suggests a major repair, management should schedule the repair.

Changing the paper or ink may not be feasible when the problem arises. Once paper or ink problems are diagnosed,

Smith dampening
system

The pumps in the
main console convert
the fluid stream into
short pulses that come
out of the spray bar as
a fine mist. The spray
bar itself is mounted
directly over the ink-
ing system rollers.

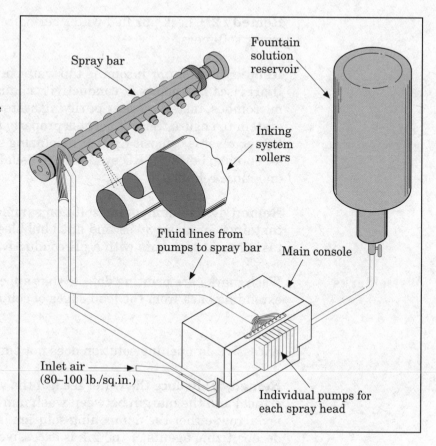

Spray bar

Fountain
solution
reservoir

Inking
system
rollers

Fluid lines from
pumps to spray bar

Main console

Inlet air
(80–100 lb./sq.in.)

Individual pumps for
each spray head

the manufacturer or supplier should be contacted immediately thereafter.

Proper plate dampening is essential to control the ink/water
balance, which is essential to high-quality printing. The following problems can result when this is not accomplished.

**Dampening
Solution
Variations**

The composition of the dampening solution varies from day
to day, even though the same proportions of concentrate and
water are mixed to make the solution.

Cause:
The chemical composition of the water used for mixing
dampening solutions changes periodically. Municipal water
that meets safety requirements for drinking is not guaran-
teed to be chemically uniform from day to day or season to
season.

Remedy 1: Switch to deep-well water if it is available.

Remedy 2: Check purified water periodically. Never use water softeners.

Remedy 3: Monitor incoming tap water hourly for one week. If pH rises 1–2 points or conductivity changes 100–200 micromhos, install a water purifying system. Monitor the system to ensure that it operates properly at all times. Either reverse osmosis (RO) or deionizing systems are acceptable; however, RO systems are usually less expensive and more reliable.

Remedy 4: Let dampening solution sample stand in clean container for about 30 second until bubbles disappear before taking measurements with a pH/conductivity meter.

Wash Marks

Wash marks are printing defects that appear as weak areas extending back from the lead edges of solids.

Cause:
Excessive dampening solution does not emulsify in the ink.

Remedy 1: Reduce the water feed. If the water control is critical and the margin between wash marks and scumming is narrow, either the dampening solution lacks adequate desensitizing agents or the ink is excessively water-repellent.

Remedy 2: Add isopropyl alcohol or alcohol substitute to the dampening solution. Make sure that the pH of acidic dampening solution is below 5.0. Adding up to 1 fl. oz. (29.6 ml) of pure 14° Baumé gum arabic per gallon may alleviate wash marks.

Snowflaky Solids

Black solids appear gray, and color solids are weak. Under magnification, solids appear uneven and full of tiny white specks.

Cause A:
Too much dampening solution; the excess emulsifies in the ink. When the ink film is split, water droplets are exposed. These droplets prevent uniform ink transfer to the paper.

Remedy: Reduce the water feed. If ink on the rollers appears to be waterlogged (greatly shortened by the moisture), change to a more water-resistant ink.

Photomicrograph of a
snowflaky solid

Cause B:
The temperature of the cooling water circulating through the
ink oscillators is too low — below 70°F (21°C). In humid
weather, this can cause moisture to condense on the ink
oscillators and promote emulsification and waterlogging.

Remedy: Raise the temperature of the cooling water.

Cause C:
The ink picks up too much dampening solution and is prone
to emulsification.

Remedy: Change to a more water-resistant ink that is compatible with the dampening solution being used.

Cause D:
Inadequate plate-to-blanket, blanket-to-substrate, and/or
roller-to-plate pressure.

Remedy: Check packing and roller settings. Correct to the
manufacturer's specifications.

**Scum Streaks
(around the
cylinder)**

Cause A:
Dirty or worn dampener or ductor roller covers or ink
buildup on brush prevent uniform dampening across the
press.

Remedy 1: Wash dampener or ductor roller covers to remove
ink accumulation. Replace threadbare roller covers.

Remedy 2: Use parchment paper dampener covers. These covers require specific rollers.

Remedy 3: Check for ink buildup on brush, and clean if necessary.

Cause B:
Greasing of the fountain roller or distributing roller can prevent uniform dampening across the press, because greasy rollers cannot hold a continuous film of water.

Remedy: Scrub fountain and distributing rollers. Apply a proprietary desensitizing solution, and buff the rollers dry.

CAUTION: Wear personal protection equipment as specified by the Material Safety Data Sheets.

Cause C:
Nonuniform pressure of dampening rollers against the plate causes uneven wear.

Remedy 1: Reset dampening rollers under uniform pressure from end to end. After they are set, the rollers should never be reversed end for end.

Remedy 2: Check the trueness of the dampeners. If a spindle or stock is bent, it should be straightened and the roller re-covered.

Scum Streaks (across the plate)

Scum streaks across the plate are usually due to lack of sufficient moisture or to excessive plate wear.

Cause A:
Bouncing dampening or inking form rollers. Rollers that are set too hard against the plate bounce when they pass over the cylinder gap and strike the lead edge of the plate. The impact rapidly wears the front edge of the plate, producing a scum streak.

Remedy: Reset the dampening rollers to the proper pressure.

Cause B:
Out-of-round or excessively hard form rollers abrade the plate.

Remedy: Replace out-of-round rollers. Deglaze, regrind, or replace hard rollers. Check the press manufacturer's recommended roller durometer measurements.

NOTE: Other causes of scumming are listed in Chapter 4.

Water Streaks

Cause:
The ductor roller strikes the distributor roller, producing a bead of water.

Remedy: Adjust the ductor to lighter contact with the distributor.

Plate Scum (overall)

The plate may develop a general scum after the job has been running for a while.

Scumming due to insufficient acid, gum, or both in the dampening solution

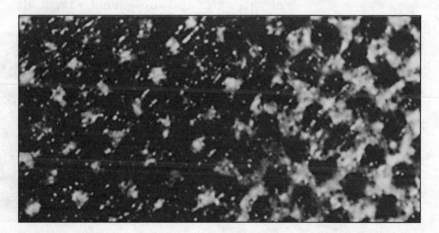

Cause A:
Insufficient acid, gum, or both in the dampening solution.

Remedy: Reformulate the dampening solution.

Cause B:
Fountain solution concentrate too strong.

Remedy 1: Check concentration using pH/conductivity meter.

Remedy 2: As a starting point, follow manufacturer's recommendations when mixing dampening solution.

NOTE: For other causes of plate scumming, refer to Chapter 6.

Halftone Sharpening

Halftone dots become sharper (smaller), and highlight dots disappear during the course of the run. The dots cannot be recovered.

Cause:
Excessive acid in the dampening solution undercuts the image areas of the plate.

Remedy: Remake the plate, and adjust the pH and conductivity values of the dampening solution.

NOTE: Refer to Chapter 6 for other causes of image failure.

White Spots (fiber-shaped)

Fiber-shaped white spots appear in printed solids when cellulose fibers adhere to the plate or blanket. These fibers absorb water and subsequently repel ink.

Spots on a printed signature

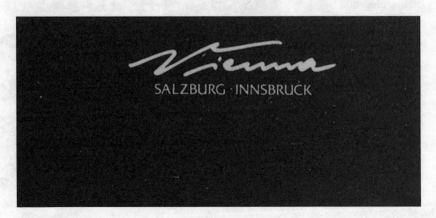

Cause
Fibers release from fabric or paper dampener roller covers. These covers eventually shed their nap fibers as a result of wear or mildew. Nap fibers are two to four times longer than paper fibers. Nap fibers can also be identified by laboratory testing.

Remedy 1: Re-cover the dampener and ductor rollers.

Remedy 2: Use parchment paper dampener covers, which do not shed fibers. These covers require frequent replacement and are to be used with specific rollers.

Remedy 3: Run bareback dampening form rollers with a durometer from 20 to 25.

Image Wear (plate)

Cause A:
Too much gum in the dampening solution.

Remedy: Re-etch the plate and rub up the image areas with ink. Turn off the dampening solution, drain the fountain, and refill the fountain with tap water. If this revives the image, replace the tap water with dampening solution that contains less gum arabic.

NOTE: UV inks more readily dissolve image areas from plates.

Cause B:
Too much acid in the dampening solution. This condition is indicated by roller stripping or the tendency of the plate to scum prior to the loss of the image.

Remedy: Replace the dampening solution with one of a higher pH.

Plate Scumming or Tinting

Cause:
Dampening solution extracts an emulsifying or sensitizing agent from the paper coating. This condition is proved if running another paper stops the tinting.

Remedy 1: Stiffen the ink as much as possible or run a stiffer ink. Consult your ink supplier if necessary.

Remedy 2: Switch paper.

Nondrying Ink

The ink fails to dry rub-resistant.

Cause A:
Too much acid in the dampening solution. Acid can retard or prevent drying of inks that contain drying oil and drier.

Remedy: Increase the dampening solution pH.

Cause B:
Excessive water in the dampening solution.

Remedy 1: Reduce the flow of the dampening solution.

Remedy 2: Reformulate the dampening solution.

Cause C:
Underexposure of UV ink to the UV drying lamps.

Remedy: Increase UV exposure, or decrease the ink film thickness.

Cause D:
Web exit temperature and chill roll temperature are set incorrectly.

Remedy: For details on setting web and chill roll temperatures, see Chapter 10.

6   Plate Problems

The lithographic printing plate consists of image and non-image areas that are on essentially on the same plane; that is, they are *planographic*. The image areas are neither raised as in letterpress, nor depressed as in gravure printing. Image and nonimage areas are chemically differentiated. Image areas accept ink and repel water; nonimage areas accept water and, therefore, repel ink.

The first metal lithographic plates had image areas that were hand-drawn using crayon or tusche, or were hand-transferred from ink images on stone. Printers later discovered that images could be photographically produced by exposing plates with light-sensitive coatings through negatives or positives. The *photolithographic* method greatly improved the quality of halftones and became the exclusive platemaking method.

Surface Plates

Surface plates are made by covering a clean metal plate with a light-sensitive coating, exposing through film, developing to remove the coating from the nonimage areas, and then desensitizing the nonimage areas.

Cross section of a surface plate

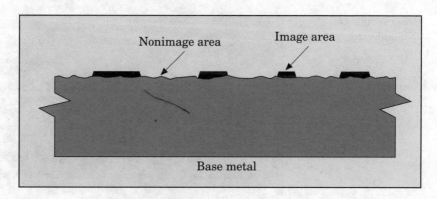

Nonimage area   Image area

Base metal

Presensitized surface plates. Presensitized surface plates are grained, ungrained, or anodized aluminum plates that have been sensitized with photopolymers and diazo compounds. They are purchased ready for exposure.

Wipe-on plates. Wipe-on plates are grained aluminum plates that must be sensitized with diazo compounds by the printer. Wipe-on plates are used primarily by newspapers and exhibit moderate durability.

Bimetal and multimetal plates. Plates of more than one metal have image and nonimage areas that are distinguished by different metals — aluminum or stainless steel for non-image areas and copper for image areas. They are presensitized, either negative- or positive-working.

Negative-working (bimetal) plates consist of a stainless-steel or aluminum base to which copper is electroplated. These presensitized plates are exposed through negatives, developed to bare the copper in the nonimage areas, then etched to remove the copper from these areas, leaving copper on the image areas.

Cross section of a bimetal plate

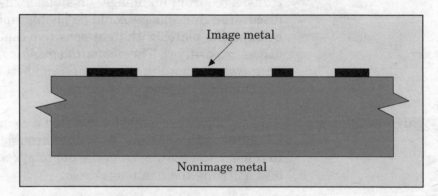

Cross section of a trimetal plate

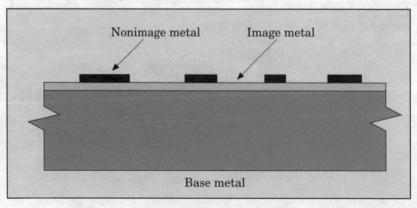

Positive-working plates are similar to negative-working plates, except that the coating is softened, or solubilized, by light. They are exposed through positives, developed to bare the copper in the nonimage areas, and etched to remove copper from nonimage areas only.

Paper (or plastic) plates. Two general varieties of paper (or plastic) plates are available: *direct-image* and *presensitized*. Such plates are used principally on offset duplicators, but are available in sizes up to about 40×54 in. (1,016×1,372 mm). Paper plates are unsuitable for use on web offset presses, because they wear quickly and tend to stretch when dampened. Thus, they should not be used when register tolerance is critical.

Laser-Imaged Plates

Laser-imaged plates are directly imaged by exposure with lasers. Because no film is used, this process completely bypasses the normal operations involved with camera and image assembly.

With advances in imaging technology, a number of lithographic printing plates are now exposed in an imagesetter or platesetter using digitally driven, low-power lasers. This class of plate is called a *direct-digital plate* because it is exposed directly from digital data, instead of being exposed through a film intermediate. This technology is usually referred to as *direct-to-plate* or *computer-to-plate* (CTP) technology.

Several different approaches to CTP technology have been announced including silver-based, electrophotographic-based, and photopolymer coatings that can be sensitized to the three dominant lasers in use today (laser diode for infrared, argon ion for blue-green, and helium neon for red) with coating sensitivities that satisfy graphic arts imaging speeds.

Waterless Plates

Plates for waterless lithography are constructed with an aluminum base, a primer, a photopolymer layer, an ink-repellent silicone rubber layer, and a transparent protective film on top. The plate can be hand- or machine-developed in a special processor. Care must be taken when handling the plates; any scratches in the silicone rubber layer become an unwanted image area.

A positive-working waterless plate is processed by first exposing it to UV light through a film positive in a vacuum frame. The exposure causes the silicone rubber layer to bind to the photopolymer layer in the nonimage area. The top pro-

The Toray Waterless
Plate
*Courtesy Toray
Marketing & Sales
(America), Inc.*

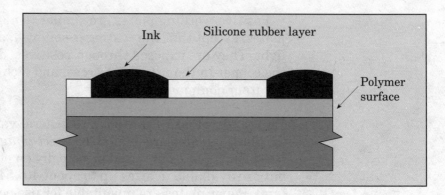

tective layer is then peeled off, and a developer that removes the silicone rubber layer from the photopolymer layer in the image areas is applied to the plate surface.

Processing of negative-working plates begins in the same way. However, with a negative-working plate, exposure to UV light through a film negative *weakens* the bonds between the photopolymer layer and the silicone rubber layer in the exposed image areas. After the exposure, the protective cover film is peeled off and a pretreatment solution is applied. This solution strengthens the binding between the silicone rubber layer and the photopolymer layer in the plate's unexposed nonimage areas. The silicone rubber layer is then removed from the photopolymer image layer in the plate's exposed areas.

Testing at GATF has proven that the waterless process produces a sharper image than conventional plates does. The waterless plate, presently, has a shorter run life than comparable conventional plates. Runs exceeding 50,000 impressions are uncommon with many waterless plates, which is not long enough for most web pressruns.

**Cost and
Longevity**

Different plates vary widely in cost and durability; therefore, they are usually selected according to run length.

Plate	Maximum Run Length
Presensitized Paper or Plastic	20,000
Direct-image Paper	10,000
Presensitized Aluminum	1,000,000
Wipe-on	200,000
Baked Presensitized	1,000,000
Bimetal	1,000,000+

Regardless of the plate being used, plate life and print quality depend on correct preparation and proper handling on press. Rollers must be properly set; cylinder packings and pressures must be correct; press operators must properly gum and wash plates.

The following section lists the most common plate problems, their probable causes, and remedies to overcome or avoid each problem. Some remedies may not be applicable under certain conditions. For example, the plate bending device may not have a vacuum hold-down; the plates may come from a trade shop or an outside supplier.

Some chronic plate problems can only be overcome by changing or modifying equipment. Where a chronic problem involves platemaking techniques, management should meet with the platemaking department or plate supplier to solve and eliminate the problem.

Changing the paper or ink may not be feasible when the problem arises. Once paper or ink problems are diagnosed, the manufacturer or supplier should be contacted immediately thereafter.

For details on paper problems and proper paper handling, consult Chapter 8. The dampening solution pH, conductivity, and percent of alcohol (if used) should be monitored by a quality control system. The following plate problems are those that are most likely to occur on web offset presses.

Improper Roll-Up

The plate image refuses to roll up properly.

Cause A:
Gum or finisher has dried hard over all or part of the image area and is accepting water instead of ink.

Remedy 1: Wet-wash the plate. Hot water and/or gum may help if the gum has been on the plate for a long time.

Remedy 2: Replace the plate. When gumming plates by hand, be sure that they are promptly buffed dry with cheesecloth. Always follow the manufacturer's instructions, using the recommended chemicals.

Cause B:
Ink or image lacquer has dried hard on the image areas and does not accept ink.

Remedy 1: Wash the plate with a cleaner that is recommended by the manufacturer.

Remedy 2: Lacquer the plate with a wipe-on lacquer or additive plate developer. Make sure that the lacquer is compatible with the plate coating.

Remedy 3: Replace the plate.

Scumming

Nonimage areas become greasy and ink-receptive.

Cause A:
Improperly formulated dampening solution.

Remedy: Replace the dampening solution with solution that has been mixed according to the manufacturer's instructions.

Ink scum

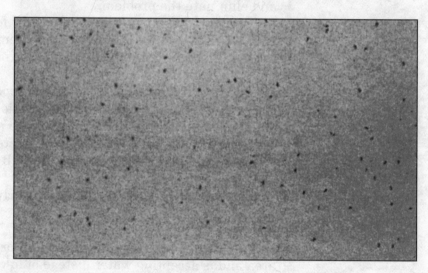

Cause B:
Dirty or worn dampener covers.

Remedy: Clean or re-cover the dampening rollers. Wet-washing may save the plate.

Cause C:
Running too much ink on halftones causes ink to spread, which eventually sensitizes nonimage areas.

Remedy: Run a thinner film of more highly pigmented ink.

Cause D:
Abrasive paper particles pile on the blanket and abrade the plate.

Remedy 1: Run a higher grade of paper.

Remedy 2: Add nonpiling agent to the dampening solution.

Remedy 3: Reduce the flow of dampening solution to a minimum; add more concentrate, gum arabic, and/or alcohol or alcohol substitute as needed to keep nonimage areas of the plate clean at reduced dampening levels.

Remedy 4: Reduce the plate-to-blanket pressures on blanket-to-blanket presses; if an impression cylinder is involved, check the impression-to-paper pressure.

Remedy 5: If piling occurs mostly on the first unit, increase the flow of dampening solution to help remove debris from the paper.

Cause E:
Oxidation of aluminum plates. Oxidation scum appears as a multitude of fine sharp dots or doughnut-shaped spots. Scum most commonly appears in areas that have stood in contact with moist dampening rollers. A plate may oxidize if it dries too slowly, or if it is stored in a damp place prior to processing or between pressruns. A plate may also oxidize if the press is stopped during a run before the plates have dried. This problem usually occurs on aluminum plates; however, it may also occur on anodized plates.

Remedy: Observe recommended plate handling procedures. Store plates in a dry place. During platemaking, dry plates quickly with cheesecloth. Raise the form rollers from the plate during a shutdown, and idle the press until the plate dries.

Cause F:
Improperly functioning dampening and/or inking rollers may result in scum streaks across or around the plate.

Remedy: Check pressure, cleanliness, trueness, and overall condition of inking and dampening rollers. Refer to the "Roller and Blanket Streaks" section of Chapter 4. Also review "Scum Streaks" in Chapter 5.

Cause G:
The plate was improperly desensitized.

Remedy 1: Use the recommended plate cleaner or desensitizer. Be sure to dry the etch thoroughly before washing it from the plate.

Remedy 2: Replace the plate.

Cause H:
Plate preexposed (fogged) in prepress.

Remedy 1: Keep plates stored in boxes under light-safe conditions.

Remedy 2: Install proper safelighting in platemaking.

Cause I:
Ink is too soft or greasy.

Remedy: Replace or stiffen the ink.

Cause J:
Counter-etching (secondary scumming) in multicolor printing. This condition occurs on the second and/or subsequent units of a multicolor press. A previously printed ink piles on a subsequent blanket and abrades the nonimage areas of the plate.

Remedy 1: Reduce the ink feed on the preceding unit; use an ink with greater color strength if necessary.

Remedy 2: Increase the acid and gum in the dampening solution of the scumming plate.

Remedy 3: Clean and regum a poorly sensitized plate.

Remedy 4: Move the ink that is causing the counter-etching to the last unit.

Cause K:
Greasy metering roller in the dampening system.

Remedy 1: Clean metal rollers in the system according to the manufacturer's instructions.

Remedy 2: Replace the ink and/or reformulate the dampening solution to improve water pickup so that rollers stay clean.

Tinting   Nonimage areas print an overall tint or randomly tinted patches, although the plate is not greasy.

Cause A:
The nonimage areas of the plate are inadequately desensitized due to incomplete removal of the plate coating. Plate scum repeats in identical patterns from sheet to sheet; tinting (ink in dampening solution) produces different patterns from sheet to sheet. Another way to check this is to wash all tint from the plate, polish part of a blank area with a scotch stone or snakeslip, and lightly etch the entire plate. If, on resuming the run, the polished area remains clean while the surrounding area scums, the cause is residual coating. If all areas continue to tint, the cause is a breakdown of the ink into the dampening solution (Cause B). If these tests indicate the presence of a residual coating, proceed as follows:

Remedy 1: Replace the plate.

Remedy 2: Clean the plate with the recommended cleaner.

Cause B:
The ink insufficiently resists water or acid, which breaks down the ink into the dampening solution. In this case, the pattern will differ from sheet to sheet. In multicolor printing, if all inks are tinting, the cause is most likely contamination (Cause C). If one or two inks are tinting while the others are printing clean, an ink or plate problem is indicated.

Remedy 1: Replace or stiffen the ink.

Remedy 2: Increase the dampening solution pH to 4 or higher; excessive acid can break down the ink.

NOTE: Low-tack inks designed for use on large, high-speed presses are likely to break down and tint if run on small, low-speed presses.

Remedy 3: Reformulate the dampening solution so that it does not readily emulsify with the ink.

Cause C:
An emulsifying or sensitizing agent from the paper, dampening solution, blanket wash, or other source is contaminating

the system. This is a likely possibility if substituting another paper or cleaning the dampening system stops the tinting.

Remedy 1: Replace or stiffen the ink.

Remedy 2: Avoid using a wetting agent in the dampening solution. Make sure that blanket or roller washes are completely removed and that the blanket is dried to prevent contamination.

Remedy 3: Completely clean the dampening system.

Remedy 4: Use another paper.

Low-Density Printing

Cause A:
Image lacks ink affinity.

Remedy: Wet-wash the plate.

Cause B:
Excessively short or waterlogged ink is piling on the rollers, plate, and blanket.

Remedy 1: Reduce dampening solution feed to the minimum required to keep nonimage areas clean.

Remedy 2: Switch to a more water-resistant ink.

Remedy 3: Lengthen the ink by adding a suitable varnish. Consult the inkmaker.

Cause C:
Plate is starting to go blind.

Remedy: Refer to the following section: "Image Blinding."

Image Blinding

Cause A:
Too much gum in the fountain solution.

Remedy: Re-etch the plate, and rub up the image areas with press ink. Drain the dampening solution, and replace it with tap water. If this revives the image, replace the tap water with dampening solution that contains less gum arabic; if not, refer to Causes B–E.

NOTE: UV inks can dissolve the image areas from some plates.

Cause B:
The dampening solution contains too much acid and gum. The excess acidity is indicated by roller stripping or plate scumming prior to image loss.

Remedy: Replace the dampening solution with one having a higher pH value.

Cause C:
Ink is too short and lacks adequate water-resistance.

Remedy 1: Rub up the image areas.

Comparing two inks for length

Remedy 2: Consult the ink supplier about replacing or lengthening the ink.

Remedy 3: Switch to a new ink.

Cause D:
Buildup of calcium or magnesium salts or detergent on the image areas of the plate.

Remedy: Wash the plate carefully with an acidic plate cleaner or a solution of alcohol, vinegar, and water. Rub up the image with ink, AGE, or a compatible wipe-on developer to be sure that the image is ink-receptive.

Cause E:
Plate-to-blanket pressure is too great, causing plate wear. This condition may be due to a swollen or embossed blanket.

Remedy 1: Correct the plate-to-blanket pressure, and check it with a packing gauge.

Remedy 2: Replace embossed blankets.

Cause F:
Dampening solution or a water-receptive layer of ink builds up on the plate. This can occur if the ink and dampening solution are incompatible.

Remedy 1: Wash the plate with plate cleaner.

NOTE: Plate cleaner may cause roller stripping and/or glazing of rollers and blankets.

Remedy 2: Change the ink.

Remedy 3: Reformulate the dampening solution.

Image Blinding (bimetal plate)

Cause A:
The copper image on a bimetal plate has become desensitized. This could be caused by an accumulation of gum in the ink, or by a sulfur compound.

Remedy: Rub up the image areas with a commercial copper sensitizer. Wash and etch the plate.

Cause B:
Dampening solution or a water-receptive layer of ink builds up over the copper image.

Remedy: Change the ink and/or dampening solution to eliminate the insoluble salt that is formed by the interaction of the ink and dampening solution.

Grainy Halftone

Cause A:
Excessive dampening solution emulsifies in the ink, thereby shortening or waterlogging it. Droplets of emulsified dampening solution wet the paper and prevent the ink from uniformly laying on the paper.

Remedy: Reduce the flow of dampening solution. If the plate scums, it was probably desensitized improperly. Remedy scumming by re-etching and gumming on press. Before doing

A water-in-ink emulsion *(left)* and an ink-in-water emulsion

On press, water-in-ink emulsification is usually more significant of the two in its effect on the process.

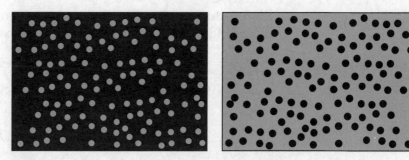

this, make sure that all image areas are protected with ink. Dry the etch thoroughly before washing it off. If this does not remove the scum, wet-wash the plate.

Cause B:
Image piling occurs when the ink is shortened by paper lint or debris, or when excessive dampening solution emulsifies into the ink.

Remedy 1: Switch to a more water-resistant paper.

Remedy 2: Wash the blanket as needed to remove paper lint.

Remedy 3: Reduce the flow of dampening solution. It may be necessary to add more concentrate and/or gum so that nonimage areas of the plate will stay clean at reduced dampening levels.

Cause C:
Inadequate squeeze between the plate and blanket.

Remedy: Check the press manufacturer's packing specifications, and make sure that the plate and blanket are properly packed for the thickness of the paper being run.

Cause D:
Coarse or uneven plate or blanket grain.

Remedy: Replace the plate or blanket with one having finer, more uniform grain.

Plate Cracking

An aluminum plate may crack along the bend in the leading or trailing edge.

Cause A:
Plate is incorrectly mounted and is not uniformly snug on the cylinder. A loosely mounted plate flexes at the bends.

Critical dimensions in plate bending

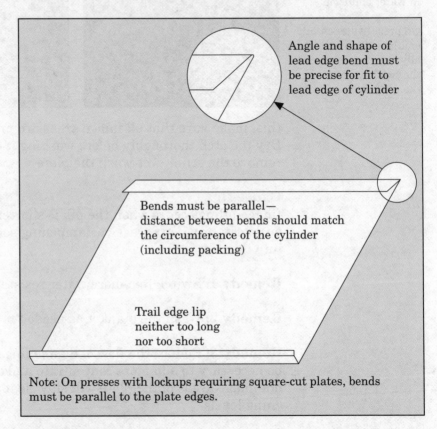

Angle and shape of lead edge bend must be precise for fit to lead edge of cylinder

Bends must be parallel— distance between bends should match the circumference of the cylinder (including packing)

Trail edge lip neither too long nor too short

Note: On presses with lockups requiring square-cut plates, bends must be parallel to the plate edges.

Remedy 1: Make sure the plate is held securely in the plate bender. A vacuum hold-down on the plate bender helps to prevent slippage. When mounting the plate on the plate cylinder, be sure that the edges are pulled down tight so that there is no bulging. The plate must be uniformly snug on the plate cylinder.

Remedy 2: Punch a small round hole at each end of the crack to keep the crack from spreading until a new plate is made.

Remedy 3: Mount the printing plate with the press on impression.

Crack at bend of
aluminum plate

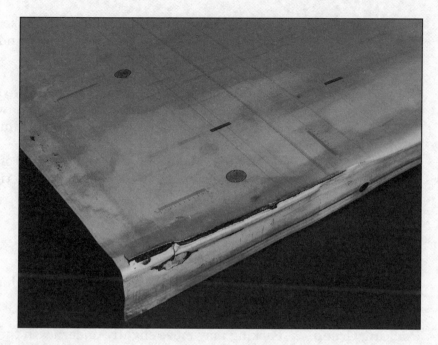

Cause B:
The plate is too long for the cylinder circumference and does
not draw down tightly against the cylinder.

Remedy 1: Compare the plate size to the press specifications.

Remedy 2: Clean dried ink from cylinder and/or plate clamping devices; the dried ink may prevent complete tightening.

Cause C:
Lead edge of the plate is bent incorrectly.

Remedy 1: Replace the plate; the lead edge must be bent so
that it corresponds to the leading edge of the plate lockup.
Also, be sure that the edge of the plate does not bottom out
in the lockup.

Remedy 2: Make sure that the lead edge bend matches the
manufacturer's recommended plate bend angle. When
switching from one thickness of plate to another, the bend
angle has to be adjusted.

Cause D:
Plate is pinched in the center, weakening the metal at that
point and causing it to crack.

Remedy 1: When bending the plate, make sure that it is squarely positioned in the plate bender and that the bending bar is straight.

Remedy 2: Check the bends to make sure that they are smooth, straight, and even. Buckles or waves create stress areas that are potential breaking points during the pressrun.

Remedy 3: Make sure that the tail edge of the plate is *squarely* positioned in the reel rod before tightening the reel rod.

Cause E:
Inadequate packing length.

Remedy: Replace packing with a sheet that covers the entire back of the plate between the bends.

Packing Creep   Packing may move slightly underneath the plate during the pressrun.

Cause:
Packing sheets slip against each other or against the cylinder. Slippage results in wrinkles that can cause the plate to bulge, thus increasing pressures and causing plate wear and cracking.

Remedy 1: Coat the back of the plate and the cylinder surface with a thin film of oil before applying the packing sheets and mounting the plate. This procedure also prevents the cylinder from rusting.

Remedy 2: Apply several stripes of grease to the back of the plate to secure the packing.

Remedy 3: Paste the leading edges of the packing sheets together when using more than one sheet under the plate.

Remedy 4: Fasten the packing sheets to the plate with spray adhesive or contact cement.

Remedy 5: Use as few sheets of packing as possible, preferably just one sheet.

Image Loss

Image loss on a presensitized plate.

Cause:
Blanket or roller wash solvents attack the image area of some unbaked positive plates. Test all solvents and cleaners on a scrap plate to ensure that they are compatible with the coating. Avoid splashing solvents on the plate.

Remedy 1: Make a new plate.

Remedy 2: Plates with thermal-setting resins can be baked before printing to improve their image durability and solvent-resistance.

Slow Roll-Up

Some baked presensitized plates are slow to roll up.

Cause:
The thermal gum was applied too thick.

Remedy 1: Wash out with manufacturer's plate cleaner or phosphoric acid solution—6 oz./gal (50 ml/l) of water.

NOTE: Consult the Material Safety Data Sheets and warning labels for the proper handling procedures and required personal protection equipment.

Remedy 2: Carefully apply asphaltum gum etch (AGE) as recommended by the manufacturer.

Scratches

The surface of the plate is linearly scratched from the front to the back edge.

Cause A:
Small abrasive particles are embedded in the ink form rollers.

Remedy 1: Locate the abrasive particle(s) and remove it from the ink roller.

Remedy 2: Remove and check all ink form rollers, and scrub them as needed.

Remedy 3: Obtain a more durable plate with a thicker anodic layer.

Cause B:
Loose metal particles released from the plate surface or edges.

Remedy: Check the plate surface and edges for loose filings before mounting it.

7   Blanket Problems

Offset printing blankets are rubber-surfaced, fabric-backed coverings that are clamped around the blanket cylinders of a printing press. The "rubber" surface is actually a synthetic polymer. Blankets receive images from the plates and transfer them to the substrate (paper). They are capable of receiving and transferring very fine images, up to 600-line/in. (240-line/cm) halftones. Combining the lithographic process with the offset method provides a low-cost printing technique that produces excellent print quality.

Compressible and **noncompressible (conventional) blankets** are available to the press operator. Blanket surfaces are formulated to meet the special requirements of ink formulations and solvents.

The reaction of a compressible blanket when out of contact with the plate *(top)* and when in contact with the plate *(bottom)*

The thickness of the rubber surface does not change. Rather, the effects of pressure are absorbed by the compressible layer.

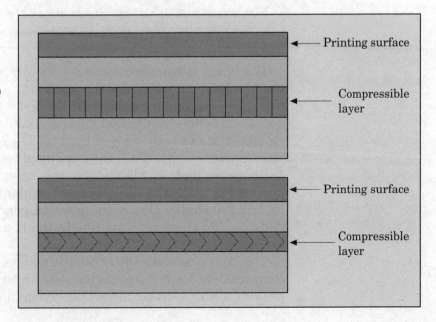

Printing surface

Compressible layer

Printing surface

Compressible layer

The displacement of conventional *(top)* and compressible blankets *(bottom)* at impact point

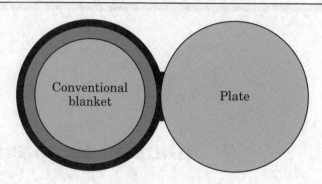

The conventional blanket bulges at impact point. Rubber displaces rather than compresses and will bulge when subjected to pressure. Because of this displacement, the surface speed of the conventional blanket is slightly different than the surface speed of the plate. One possible result is slurring.

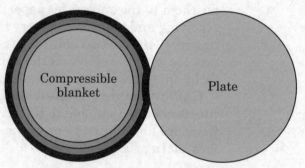

With a compressible blanket, slight bulges do form, but to a lesser extent than with a conventional blanket.

The terms *compressible* and *noncompressible* describe how the blanket behaves under the squeezing action of the printing nips — plate/blanket nip and blanket/substrate nip. The noncompressible blanket when squeezed in a nip bulges out on either one or both sides of the nip. The materials cannot be compressed; therefore, they are displaced.

Excessive plate-to-blanket squeeze causes a rubbing action against the plate and the paper as the blanket tries to recover its original shape. This rubbing action generally increases dot gain and shortens plate life. In the blanket/substrate nip, excessive squeeze slurs the print.

The layers beneath the synthetic polymer surface of a compressible blanket are porous; the air in these layers compresses in the printing nips. This design accommodates greater interference (within reason) that usually improves ink transfer without excessive dot gain.

Blankets are made to work well with coated papers. UV inks require the use of specially formulated compressible or noncompressible blankets. The synthetic polymer in the face of the blanket is formulated to meet these requirements. Quick-release blankets may have a ground or roughened surface to reduce the pulling force of the ink in the nip. These blankets permit the press to be run at high speed without damaging the paper. High pressures are required to transfer ink from plate to blanket and blanket to paper; however, excessive squeeze can reduce the quick-release properties. Furthermore, excessive pressure produces dot gain in halftones, interferes with web feed, and causes web breaks. Consult the blanket manufacturer to determine the appropriate uses of a specific blanket.

Comparison of squeeze required to obtain equal pressures for printing

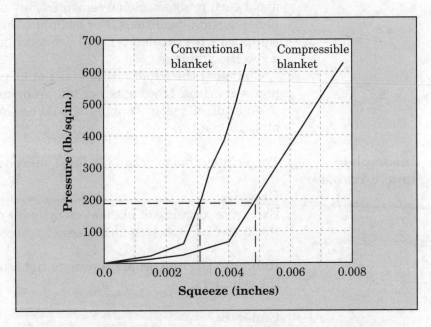

Mounting tension and running compaction reduce the thickness of a new blanket during the first few thousand impressions. If the blanket thickness is measured with a micrometer, and the calculated thickness of packing is added to give 0.003–0.004 in. (0.08–0.10 mm) of squeeze, the image may no longer completely transfer ink after a few thousand impressions. Check the blanket with a packing gauge to determine how much it has compressed. Add packing to raise the blanket to its original height.

Packing requirements vary, depending on the blanket. Assuming that press conditions require pressure of 190 lb./sq. in. (134 g/mm^2), approximately 0.003 in. (0.08 mm) of squeeze will be required with a conventional blanket to supply the desired pressure. With a compressible blanket, 0.005 in. (0.12 mm) of squeeze is required to supply the equivalent pressure.

Blanket problems are typically attributable to incompatible ink, improper packing and mounting, and improper treatment of the blanket when first put on the press or during printing. Blankets are available to match almost any ink-paper combination. If either the ink or paper is changed, consult the blanket manufacturer to determine the appropriate blanket to use. The printing plate and the dampening solution may also affect blanket performance.

The following section lists the most common blanket problems, their probable causes, and remedies to overcome or avoid each problem. Some remedies may not be applicable under certain conditions. For example, the press may not be equipped with the devices that are recommended to remedy a specific problem.

Changing the paper or ink may not be feasible when the problem arises. Once paper or ink problems are diagnosed, the manufacturer or supplier should be contacted immediately thereafter.

Incomplete Image Transfer

The printed image gradually loses sharpness or solidity.

Cause A:
Excessive torquing of blanket on cylinder decreases blanket thickness; i.e., causes gauge loss.

Remedy: Use the proper torque to tighten the blankets on the cylinders.

Cause B:
The blanket compresses due to running compaction. This principally occurs with a new blanket.

Remedy: Check the height of the blanket with a packing gauge, and add packing as required.

Cause C:
Increased squeeze caused by a blanket that has swelled. This may be due to a blanket wash that evaporates too slowly

and/or has too high a KB (kauri-butanol) number. Using UV inks also causes blanket swelling.

Remedy 1: Check the height of the blanket with a packing gauge. Remove packing to compensate for the increased squeeze.

Remedy 2: Use solvent- and oil-resistant blankets that are designed to print heatset inks.

Remedy 3: Use a blanket wash that evaporates faster and has a lower KB number. Consult with the blanket supplier.

Cause D:
The ink and blanket are incompatible (e.g., using a UV ink with a conventional blanket). This can cause embossing and create excessive pressure in the image areas.

Remedy 1: Switch to a blanket that is compatible with the ink.

Remedy 2: Replace the ink.

Cause E:
The blanket surface has become glazed and hard; therefore, it no longer accepts ink. Glazing may result from accumulated gum, paper coating, water-receptive salts, dried ink, or dried varnish.

Remedy 1: Use a blanket wash that completely removes gum, paper coating, ink, and varnish.

Remedy 2: Sponge the blanket with water during every washup. Scrub with the recommended solvent and/or a commercial glaze remover, using a nylon scrubbing pad.

Remedy 3: Discard the blanket.

Cause F:
Excessive bearer pressure generates heat, and the bearers expand.

Remedy: Allow the bearers to cool. Check the height of the plate and blanket, and reset bearer pressures.

Ghosting

A ghost image appears from a previously printed job.

Cause A:
The blanket is embossed, because it has absorbed ink vehicle from the previously printed job.

Remedy: Install a new blanket.

NOTE: Thoroughly clean the old blanket with blanket wash, and hang it in a dark place. Do not reuse the blanket until the absorbed oil has had adequate time to diffuse through the rubber. Make sure that the embossing is gone.

Cause B:
The blanket is debossed, because the ink vehicle has extracted soluble materials from it.

Remedy 1: Install a new blanket.

Remedy 2: Change to ink that is compatible with the blanket.

Picking

Paper sticks to or is picked by printing areas of the blanket.

Cause:
The blanket surface has swelled and become tacky. This is caused by washing the blanket with solvent that is too strong. Dampening solutions with high concentrations of alcohol may also deposit gum on the blanket.

Remedy: Wash the blanket with water and a compatible solvent. Consult the blanket manufacturer.

NOTE: Never use sulfur or a sulfur compound or a chlorinated compound on a blanket when printing with bimetal plates. They blind the copper image areas.

Uneven Impression

Images that print unevenly require excessive pressure to transfer evenly.

Cause A:
Nonuniform blanket thickness. Locate low spots using the following procedure:
1. Remove the plate and packing.
2. Wash plate cylinder, and replace the plate and packing.

3. Run the press with a thin ink film on the form rollers. Lower an ink form roller until it lightly contacts the plate. If the plate inks up evenly, check the blanket for depressed areas that have not received ink.

4. Put the press on impression, and run it for several revolutions. Ink will not transfer from the plate to depressed areas of the blanket.

Remedy 1: Replace the blanket.

Remedy 2: Establish thickness tolerances with the blanket supplier. Measure several areas of each blanket with a deadweight bench micrometer. If the blanket thickness varies beyond the acceptable limits, return it to the supplier.

Remedy 3: Patch the back of the blanket with tissue that has been torn to the shape of the depressed area. Adhere the tissue with gum arabic.

Cause B:
One or more warped or dented cylinders.

Remedy 1: Replace or repair the cylinder(s).

Remedy 2: If the dent is not too deep, build up the cylinder surface with tissue torn to the shape of the depressed area. Apply tissue to the cylinder with shellac. Use fine sandpaper on a flat block to taper the edges and smooth down high spots after the shellac has dried. This procedure is recommended as a *temporary* solution.

Remedy 3: For permanent correction, metallize the cylinder and regrind it.

Smashed Blanket

The blanket surface is indented from excessive pressure or from excessive tension in the around-the-cylinder direction.

Cause A:
A foreign object passes through the press.

Remedy 1: Replace the blanket.

Remedy 2: Wash the low spot with blanket wash to swell it as much as possible.

Cause B:
Paper wraps up around the blanket or passes through the impression nip in a crumpled or wadded condition.

Remedy 1: Replace the smashed blanket.

Remedy 2: Wash the low area thoroughly with blanket wash to swell it as much as possible.

Remedy 3: Use a thicker blanket if the cylinder undercut is deep enough.

Remedy 4: If a conventional blanket was smashed, switch to a compressible blanket.

Cause C:
Excessively tightening the blanket in the clamping mechanisms creates a low spot or gauge loss where the blanket is stretched.

Remedy 1: Tighten blankets on the cylinder using a torque wrench that has been set to the blanket manufacturer's recommended tension.

Remedy 2: Replace the blanket.

Remedy 3: Wash the blanket to swell the low spots.

Streaks   Streaks appear horizontally in the printed image.

Cause A:
A loose blanket may slip on the blanket cylinder if the plate and blanket cylinders are not packed equally. The inked blanket adheres to the plate beyond the nip and slips in the around-the-cylinder direction. Higher plate-to-blanket pressure causes greater slippage.

Remedy: Tighten the blanket to the recommended torque. Check the plate and blanket heights with a packing gauge to determine the plate-to-blanket pressure. Remove excess packing.

Cause B:
The press vibrates when cylinder gaps align under pressure.

Remedy 1: Check the height of the packed blanket; remove excess packing as needed.

Remedy 2: Change to a compressible blanket.

Remedy 3: When length of print is not a consideration, move the blanket cylinder gaps "out of time" to help reduce or eliminate the bounce.

Cause C:
Blanket washer set too tight.

Remedy: Reset the blanket washer.

Slur

Cause A:
Incorrect plate and blanket packing. Where a significant difference in peripheral speed occurs between plate and blanket, the elasticity of the blanket allows it to move and distort in the plate/blanket nip when lubricated by the inked image areas.

Remedy: Use high-grade hard packing paper to pack the plate and blanket to the manufacturer's specifications.

Cause B:
On presses with back cylinders (impression cylinders), too much back-cylinder pressure causes slurring when printing on coated papers. Slur shows up on shadow tones, filling in images and causing loss of detail. Highlights are usually unaffected.

Remedy 1: Run with minimal back-cylinder pressure. Print thin ink films of high color strength.

Remedy 2: Use a compressible blanket.

Cause C:
On presses with impression (back) cylinders, the impression cylinder is free-wheeling and driven by blanket cylinder pressure against paper and cylinder.

Remedy 1: Use coated paper with less slip.

Remedy 2: Discuss the problem with the press manufacturer because it is related to the press design.

Cause D:
Too much plate-to-blanket pressure when running a smooth or lightly grained plate.

Remedy: Reduce plate-to-blanket squeeze to a minimum. Ungrained plates require approximately 0.003 in. (0.076 mm) of squeeze when using conventional blankets; 0.005–0.006 in. (0.13–0.15 mm) of squeeze is required when running new compressible blankets.

Cause E:
Insufficient blanket tension.

Remedy: Use a torque wrench to tighten blankets to the recommended tension.

Micrometer-adjustable torque-sensing wrench

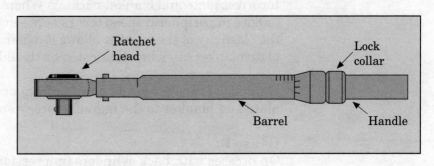

8   Paper Problems

Web offset printing papers include newsprint, offset, coated free sheet or groundwood, and super-calendered. The surface of web offset papers should resist picking and be relatively free of dust and lint. The paper should resist moisture, thus preventing dampening solution from loosening the surface fibers or coating pigment. It must also exhibit good ink-receptivity and high holdout.

Coating that has been removed from a halftone area

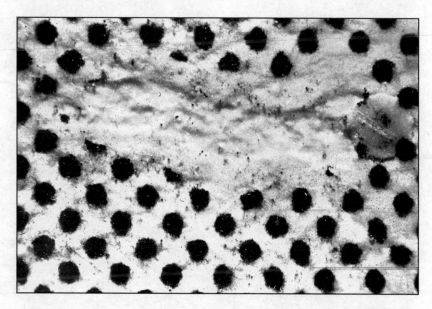

Paper is a porous material in which the pores or voids sometimes amount to half of its total volume. Its structure is determined by the materials used in its manufacture and by the forces that enter into the papermaking operation. Important physical characteristics of paper are thickness, strength, and surface quality. Other structural characteristics that are of primary importance to the printer include grain, two-sidedness, and density.

Grain. Grain is a characteristic of all machine-made papers. It results primarily from fiber alignment during the formation or drying of the sheet. The fibers tend to align themselves parallel to the direction traveled by the wire of the paper machine. On all roll papers, grain direction is lengthwise on the web, parallel to the direction of web travel. The effects of grain on paper properties are as follows:

- Paper tears and folds more easily in the grain direction than across the grain.
- Paper exhibits greater stiffness and higher tensile strength in the grain direction.
- Paper absorbs or gives off moisture with changes in atmospheric humidity. When in contact with a wet blanket, passing through a dryer, and running in contact with chill rolls, it expands or contracts more in the cross direction than in the grain direction.

Paper cut in the direction of the paper grain *(top)* and across it

Paper is stiffer in the direction of the grain than across the grain, and folds are cleanest when made parallel to the grain direction

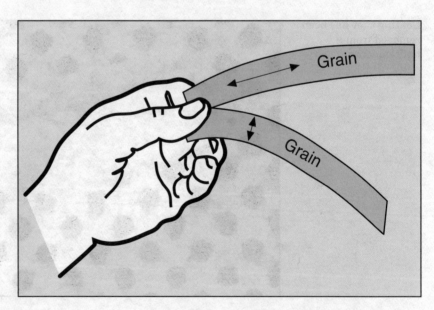

Two-sidedness. Because paper is first formed on the wire screen of a paper machine, its two sides are different in structure. The bottom or wire side has a porosity somewhat different from that of the top or felt side and is somewhat different in composition. The fibers on the wire side line up more completely in the machine direction than those on the felt side; thus, the finished sheet is two-sided.

The wire side of uncoated paper has an open structure, contains less size and filler and fewer short fibers, and has a more pronounced grain. The felt side has a closer structure and less grain, because the fibers are more completely interwoven. The sophistication of modern papermaking machines has greatly reduced two-sidedness so that both sides of the stock print similarly. Paper made on a twin-wire machine has two wire sides.

Density. Density is the weight of paper relative to its volume. Dense papers are compact, and their fibers are strongly bonded together. Surface-sizing and supercalendering also increase density. In soft, bulky, porous papers, individual fibers can swell or shrink without so much change in the overall dimensions of the sheet. The dimensional stability of paper, therefore, closely relates to density. It is related to the amount of change in the dimensions of a sheet for a given change in its moisture content.

Nonuniform density in a web can cause tension variations. Especially in uncoated stocks, uneven density can also lead to nonuniform ink absorption (mottle).

Performance requirements. Papers used in web offset come in a wide variety of classifications, grades, and finishes. Their basis weights range from about 25 lb. to more than 100 lb. — basic size 25×38 in. (37–148 g/m^2). Heavier weights can be run but do not handle well in folders and are usually delivered in sheets. Heavier-weight coated papers are also more prone to blistering. Lighter-weight papers are difficult to run because of their lower tensile strength and lower stress resistance. For satisfactory performance in web offset, papers should meet the following basic requirements:

Cleanliness. Paper must be free from dust, dirt, and debris that inevitably cause printing defects and require downtime for a press washup.

Roll winding. Rolls must be properly wound to ensure good performance on press. Tension variations in the unwinding roll cause erratic longitudinal and lateral movements, which result in misregister or web breaks.

Flatness. Webs should be flat enough to pass through the printing nips without wrinkling or excessively distorting.

Flatness is only in part achieved through proper press settings. Webs develop wavy edges as a result of varying moisture content or basis weight. These webs can be substantially improved on the press by increasing the distance traveled and the tension between the roll and the first printing unit.

Moisture content. Web stress is constant on the press when tension settings have been completed. The forces applied to the web stay the same during the pressrun. As the web picks up moisture from unit to unit, its dimensional stability changes. Tension must be adjusted to maintain register.

Nonuniformity in moisture content is more frequent across the web width. Variation in this direction can result in one or both edges of the web running tight while the center runs baggy or vice versa. This can lead to localized misregister, wrinkling, and doubling in the loose parts of the web. Modern infeed tension control devices improve the runnability of such a roll by subjecting it to maximum pre-stressing before it reaches the printing units. Alternatively, the web may be run through the longest possible lead in the infeed under the high tension.

Moisture content should be uniform throughout the roll; it should also be as high as possible—but within web paper specifications to lessen the chance of blistering in the dryer. The dryer drives most of the moisture out of the web. Dry paper cracks easily in the folder, and delivered signatures are extremely dry. If a bound book has low moisture, it will pick up atmospheric moisture, turning the edges wavy. Remoisturizing restores adequate moisture content to the paper, ensuring that the delivered signatures remain dimensionally stable. This process also reduces static electricity in the web.

Note that many of the sheetfed printer's concerns about conditioning paper to pressroom atmosphere do not apply to the web printer. If wrappings are left on the roll as long as possible, atmospheric humidity has little effect on roll moisture content. The edges of the roll are tightly wound and relatively impervious to atmospheric moisture.

Surface strength. Surface strength is the characteristic of paper that enables it to resist external forces — chemical and mechanical — as it passes through the printing press. Diverse papers exhibit varying degrees of surface strength.

Roll condition. The condition of the paper rolls is important. They should be round and uniformly wound under proper tension, free from soft spots, welts, corrugations, and water streaks, and they should not be *starred*. Fully protect them from the atmosphere and maintain constant moisture content throughout by proper wrapping.

The wrappings should be undamaged and kept on the roll until just before it is run on the press. Several layers of paper that must be slabbed off the outside of a damaged roll represent a substantial loss, particularly on a roll of large diameter.

Damage to the wrappers on rolls of paper, which can result in loss of necessary moisture, or in too much moisture

Paper printability. Printability is the characteristic of paper that is directly related to the quality of the images printed on it. Physical and optical properties of paper and its surface affect tone and color reproduction, smoothness of print, and therefore the appearance of the printed reproduction. Diverse papers provide varying degrees of fidelity in tone and color, contrast, smoothness of halftones and solids, and clarity of detail.

The attractiveness of a printed reproduction depends on the nature of the original and the end use of the printed piece. Some subjects such as portraits, greeting cards, or abstract art appear more attractive when reproduced with the soft effects obtainable on a rough vellum stock. Other subjects such as machinery, furniture, or food illustrations, requiring sharpness and clear detail, are best reproduced on a high-finished or coated stock.

Color. Paper can be made in almost any color. Process color reproduction should employ white paper. Any color in the paper reduces the color gamut of the reproduction. The colors affected most are those complementary to the paper color. Blue sheets reduce the clarity of yellow, and red sheets cause green to appear gray. Slight variations from white (blue-white, cream-white, or pink-white) may still produce acceptable results; however, they are visibly discernible. A white as near neutral as possible is necessary to get the maximum color gamut from any given set of process inks.

Brightness. Brightness of paper is a measure of the reflectance of blue light (at a wavelength of 457 nanometers), which provides a value indicative of the degree of bleaching. Optical brighteners that increase blue-light reflectance contribute to contrast in the printed subject — provided that the colors are limited to blue and black — and therefore to brilliance, snap, and sparkle. Brightness reduces the color gamut of yellows, reds, and greens. Variations in brightness detract from print quality, most noticeably in large areas of halftone tints.

Whiteness. Whiteness is the degree of reflectance, in *uniform* amounts, of red, green, and blue light. White objects are highly reflective. Conversely, black objects reflect little or no red, green, and blue light, although the reflectance — or the lack thereof — may be uniform.

Opacity. Opacity, the extent to which light transmission is obstructed, controls show-through of printed matter. Show-through is the lack of opacity that allows the printing on the reverse side of the sheet to be seen through the stock. Excessive show-through reduces contrast and detracts from print quality. Show-through is different from strike-through. Strike-through is excessive penetration of ink through the sheet.

Smoothness. Smoothness describes the continuous evenness of a paper's surface. Smoother paper surfaces require a thinner ink film to attain adequate coverage. A thin ink film promotes better rendition of tones, greater sharpness, and clarity of detail.

Gloss. Gloss is the property of a paper surface or a printed ink film determined by the degree to which specular reflection exceeds diffuse reflection. High-gloss papers are desirable for some applications but inappropriate for others. They enhance the brilliance and intensity of colors but are objectionable for reading matter because of glare. Paper gloss has an important effect on the gloss or finish of printed ink films. When identical ink films are printed on papers of equal ink absorbency, the ink gloss is always higher on the glossier paper.

Paper performance. Core cards for reporting roll performance should be filled out and returned to the mill. This information tracks good and poor performance. Report all problems to the mill; provide as many details as possible. Include samples that show the nature of the problem. Detailed, continuous information helps the mill to provide rolls with improved runnability and printability.

Preparing the new roll. Careful attention to makeready at the infeed can go far toward ensuring a smooth start-up and run. The roll tender should closely inspect each roll before mounting it on the press. The roll should be round. Out-of-round rolls have a higher incidence of web breaks.

Check for nicked sides and torn wrappers. A torn wrapper — even without damage to the roll underneath — indicates potential trouble. Most wrappers are moisture-proof to preserve the natural moisture content of the web (about 5%). Usually, the first part of the roll to dry out in storage is the surface near the tear. The result is uneven running tension. The best practice is to leave the body wrapper on until just before the roll is prepared for splicing.

Finally, the roll tender should check for defective roll cores. A roll with a deformed core wobbles while running, causing problems with all but the most sophisticated infeeds.

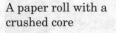

A paper roll with a crushed core

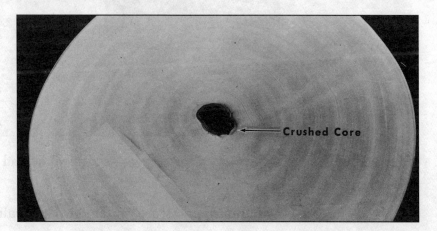

Solving Paper-Related Problems

The following section lists the most common paper problems, their probable causes, and remedies to overcome or avoid each problem. Some remedies may not be applicable under certain conditions. For example, the press may not be equipped with the devices that are recommended to remedy a specific problem.

Some chronic paper problems can only be overcome by equipment, which may not be available on press. Management should consider acquiring the equipment required to enhance the productivity of the press.

Changing the paper or ink may not be feasible when the problem arises. Once paper or ink problems are diagnosed, the manufacturer or supplier should be contacted immediately thereafter.

Telescoped Roll

A roll with progressive edge misalignment, concave or convex, due to slippage of its inner layers in the direction of its axis as a result of a thrust force on or within its body after being wound.

Cause:
Roll was wound under too little tension.

Remedy: Reject the roll, and return it and the completed roll card to the supplier.

A telescoped roll

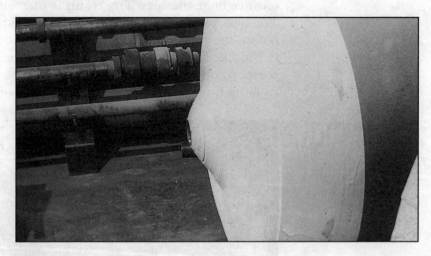

Corrugated Roll

A corrugated roll weaves as it unwinds and causes misregister.

Cause A:
Nonuniform moisture content or paper caliper.

Corrugated roll

Remedy 1: Increase the distance and number of infeed rollers between the roll stand and the first printing unit to flatten the web.

Remedy 2: Install a curved infeed roller, specifically designed to flatten wrinkled paper.

Action of a Mt. Hope curved roller in spreading or narrowing the paper web
Courtesy Mt. Hope Machinery Co.

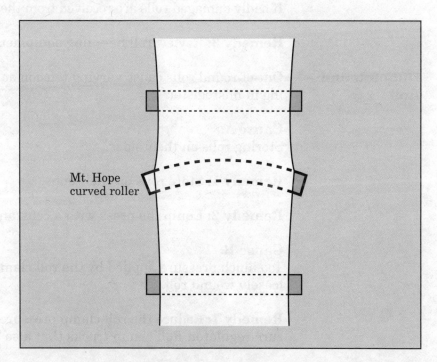

Mt. Hope
curved roller

Remedy 3: Spirally tape an infeed roller to spread and flatten the web.

Remedy 4: Equip the press with a constant-tension infeed.

Cause B:
Unwrapping rolls in a highly humid area and allowing them to stand long enough to absorb moisture from the air.

Remedy 1: Slab off the outer ¼ in. (6 mm) of paper.

Remedy 2: Remove the wrapper from a roll immediately before mounting it on the roll stand.

Dented Roll

Dents or cuts on the ends of a roll initiate web breaks.

Cause:
Careless handling or accident.

Remedy 1: If the dent is not too deep, sand, grind, or cut it out until the edges of the paper are smooth.

Remedy 2: If the dent is deep, print down to the dent, stop the press, slab off the dented area, resplice, and resume printing. If badly damaged rolls are received from the mill, return them.

Remedy 3: Review roll handling equipment and procedures.

Out-of-Round Roll

Out-of-round rolls cause varying tension at the infeed, resulting in misregister.

Cause A:
Storing rolls on their sides.

Remedy 1: Store rolls on their ends.

Remedy 2: Equip the press with a constant-tension infeed.

Cause B:
Too much pressure applied by the roll clamp truck to a loosely wound roll.

Remedy 1: Reduce the roll clamp pressure, or install a pressure regulator. Roll clamp trucks that also apply vacuum to the roll require less clamping pressure. Equip the roll clamp truck with rubber pads.

Remedy 2: Equip the press with a constant-tension infeed.

Starred Roll

Roll is starred or wavy near the core, causing tension to vary when feeding from the starred area.

Cause:
Roll is wound under progressively higher tension at the mill.

Remedy: Reject the roll, and return it and the completed roll card to the supplier.

Wrinkles or Creases

The paper wrinkles or creases lengthwise along the web.

Cause:
The roll picked up moisture from the atmosphere.

Remedy 1: Prevention. Do not unwrap until ready to splice.

Remedy 2: Adjust the eccentric-mounted infeed roller to balance edge tension.

Remedy 3: Build up the ends of an infeed roller with tape or paper under the slack areas.

Remedy 4: Increase web tension to tighten slack edges.

Remedy 5: Equip the press with a curved infeed roller.

Tight Edge

The web pulls tight or wrinkles on one side although loose on the opposite side after each flying splice. The next roll reverses tension; the tight side becomes loose, and the loose side becomes tight.

Cause:
Rolls come from different positions of the paper machine web and have different side-to-side characteristics.

Remedy 1: Run rolls in groups, according to their machine position. Color coding identifies machine position of each roll.

Remedy 2: Reject roll.

**White Spots
(fiber-shaped)**

White fiber-shaped spots appear in solids; halftones are grainy.

Cause A:
Uncoated paper with loosely bonded surface fibers variously referred to as lint, fuzz, fluff, and whiskers. These fibers are lifted by tacky inks, even when printing a single color. Once fibers become attached to the blanket or plate, the fibers absorb moisture and repel ink.

A test for lint

Remedy 1: Reduce the tack of the ink as much as possible without affecting print quality.

Remedy 2: Install a blanket cleaner on the press.

Lint, or loose paper fibers

A solid printed on
linty paper, enlarged

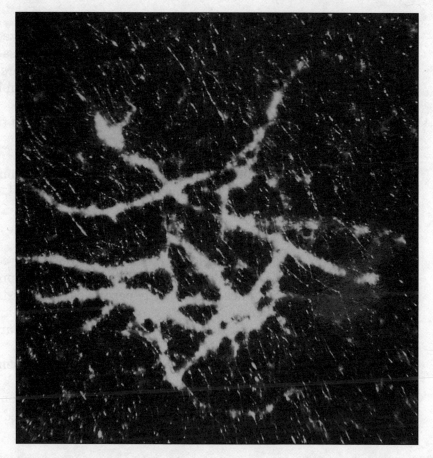

Remedy 3: Install a hickey-picking form roller, usually in the first-down position. These rollers help to dislodge lint and dust that tend to accumulate on the plates.

Remedy 4: Add 0.002-in. (0.05-mm) packing under the blanket; add 0.001 in. (0.025 mm) under each blanket of a blanket-to-blanket press. (This remedy does not eliminate linting, but the extra printing pressure improves the solids to the point that you can print the job if changing to a different paper is not an alternative.)

Remedy 5: Return paper that lints excessively to the supplier. Attach a completed core card to the roll.

Remedy 6: Install a web cleaner on the press.

Remedy 7: Retrofit the press with a Delta-style dampening system.

Cause B:
Inadequately bonded fibers of surface-sized papers are softened by the first unit of a multicolor press and lifted by the inked blanket of a subsequent unit. Fibers are held down by the starch of the surface size, rather than by hydration.

Remedy 1: Reduce the plate dampening to the minimum required to keep nonimage areas clean.

Remedy 2: Lower the dampening solution pH and add more gum to the dampening solution. This will allow less dampening solution to be run.

Cause C:
Molleton or other fabric dampening roller covers yield cotton fibers that stick to plate or blanket, thus preventing ink transfer. These fibers are generally easier to distinguish from paper fibers; usually, they are fewer in number, and their average length exceeds ⅛ in. (3 mm). Paper fibers are usually shorter.

Remedy 1: Put new covers on the dampeners.

Remedy 2: Use parchment paper dampener covers. These covers are replaced easily and do not shed fibers. They require special base rollers.

NOTE: Remedy 2 may cause surging — variations in the amount of dampening solution transferred to the plate.

Cause D:
Web cleaners that employ brushes may abrade the paper surface and loosen surface fibers.

Remedy: Set web cleaner brushes with lighter pressure on the web.

Web Break

Web breaks are a serious problem in web offset printing. They can occur anywhere on the press from the infeed to the cutoff. Web breaks result in downtime, paper waste, and often damage to the plates and blankets. Excessive tension, if uniform, is not likely to cause web breaks. Most papers have a tensile strength greater than 12 lb./in. (216 g/mm) of width. This equals approximately 432 lb. (196 kg) for a 36-in. (914-mm) web.

Cause A:
Excessive tension on one or both edges of web due to moisture loss and shrinkage. The edges of the web become tight, and the center becomes baggy. If an edge tears, a web break results.

Remedy: Prevention. Do not unwrap rolls until immediately before splicing. Make sure that the wrappers of stored rolls are intact.

Cause B:
Paper defects (fiber cuts, hair cuts, wire holes, wrinkles, slime spots, foam spots, calender cuts) start a tear that may result in a web break.

Remedy: Return defective paper, and run a new roll.

Common web defects
Courtesy Kimberly-Clark Corp.

Calender cut

Fiber cut

Hair cut

Wire hole

Cause C:
Roll end is dented or cut. Such defects can start tears that result in web breaks.

Remedy: If the dent is not too deep, sand, grind, or cut it out until the edges of the paper are smooth. If badly damaged rolls are received from the mill, return them.

Cause D:
Bad splice. Web breaks can occur if the draw across the splice is uneven.

Remedy: Resplice the roll. If this is a recurring problem, contact the mill; provide evidence of the bad splice.

Cause E:
Printing units or other press elements may be out of line. Misalignment is indicated if a proportionally large number of web breaks occur in one section of the press. Diagonal wrinkles in any web span indicate misalignment of press elements.

Remedy: Have the press alignment checked and corrected if necessary.

Rough Printed Solids

Solids on uncoated paper may look and feel rough.

Cause:
Poorly bonded surface fibers are raised but not picked from the paper by the inked blanket. This problem can occur in single- or multicolor printing.

Remedy 1: Reduce the ink tack as much as possible without affecting print quality.

Remedy 2: Install a hickey-picking form roller in the first-down position. These rollers help to dislodge lint and dust that accumulate on the plates.

Remedy 3: Reject paper that lints excessively. Fill out the core card, and contact the supplier.

White Spots (non-fiber-shaped)

Spots that are not fiber-shaped repeat on consecutive sheets and increase in number during the run.

Cause A:
Loose slitter dust, cutter dust, or dryer scale on the web.

Remedy 1: Install a vacuum web cleaner. Web cleaners must be accurately set and equipped with an operable brush.

Remedy 2: Wet-wash the ends of the roll with a sponge before running.

NOTE: Web cleaners may produce dirt on coated stock.

Cause B:
Flakes of coating or particles are picked from the paper surface. To distinguish them from loose dust particles, examine the previously printed signatures or sheets; locate the one on which the spot first appeared. Examine the spot with a magnifier. If the paper surface is ruptured, the paper was picked. Otherwise, loose dust caused the spot.

Remedy 1: Reduce the ink tack as much as possible without affecting print quality. If this does not help, the paper may be unsuitable for web offset.

Remedy 2: Use a hickey-picking roller to help remove and store particles that have adhered to the plate.

Remedy 3: Retrofit the press with a Delta-style dampening system.

Picking or Splitting

Picking is the rupturing of small areas of the paper surface that occurs when the pulling force of the ink exceeds the surface or internal bond strength of the paper. **Splitting** is the

Paper split in printed solid due to paper weakness or excessive ink tack.

peeling of larger areas of the paper surface, which stick to the blanket. Splitting usually causes a web break. Picking and splitting almost always occur in solids.

Cause A:

The surface or internal bond strength of the paper is too low or the bonding of coating to the base stock is too weak. Have the paper tested; if pick resistance is normal, see Cause B. If pick resistance is weak, try the following remedies:

Picking of coated paper

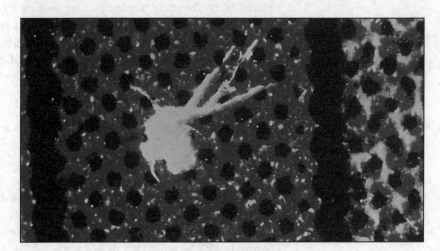

Remedy 1: Change to a more pick-resistant paper.

Remedy 2: Increase the ink film thickness; maintain acceptable color.

Remedy 3: Reduce the ink tack with a reducer or solvent as recommended by the inkmaker.

Remedy 4: Increase the flow of dampening solution.

Remedy 5: Slightly increase the temperature of the ink train rollers.

Remedy 6: Reduce press speed.

Cause B:

Paper with good pick resistance when dry is weakened by moisture in multicolor presswork. The first-down color prints OK, but the inked blankets of the subsequent printing units pick the paper.

Remedy 1: Reduce the pH to allow for lower levels of dampening on the plate and reduce the printing pressure to a minimum on all units. It may be necessary to add gum or concentrate to the dampening solution to keep nonimage areas of the plate clean at reduced dampening levels.

Remedy 2: Change to a better-sized (more moisture-resistant) paper.

Delamination

Delamination is the removal of the paper surface that occurs on one side of the web in the direction of web travel. The delaminated area has ragged edges.

Cause:
Sharp flexing of the web beyond the impression nip caused by the web simultaneously adhering to both blankets, which are printing heavy solids.

Remedy 1: Print with quick-release blankets.

Remedy 2: Reduce the ink tack by adding a reducer as recommended by the inkmaker.

Remedy 3: Reduce the ink tack by increasing the flow of dampening solution.

Remedy 4: Reduce the press speed.

Remedy 5: Run the wire side of the web to the form with the heaviest ink coverage.

Remedy 6: Add more fountain solution concentrate or an alcohol substitute to the dampening solution.

Remedy 7: Check the squeeze between blankets, and reduce the pressure if necessary.

Piling (coated paper)

Paper coating piles on the blankets in nonimage areas. Accumulated coating causes halftones to become sandy and highlight dots to disappear.

Cause:
Running coated paper that is hypersensitive to moisture.

Blanket piling

Remedy 1: Avoid coated papers with poor wet rub resistance, unless they have run successfully during press tests.

Remedy 2: Reduce the amount of dampening solution on all units. It may be necessary to add gum or concentrate to keep nonimage areas of the plate clean at reduced dampening levels.

Remedy 3: Use less alcohol substitute and/or increase the pH of the dampening solution.

Piling (uncoated paper)

Uncoated paper piles on blankets.

Cause:
Fibers and filler are pulled from the paper and accumulate on the blanket.

Remedy 1: Reduce the ink tack.

Remedy 2: Increase blanket packing by 0.002 in. (0.05 mm). Increased pressure helps to scrub accumulated material from the blanket.

Remedy 3: Increase the flow of dampening solution to lubricate the blanket. **NOTE:** This remedy could make the situation worse.

Remedy 4: Add a nonpiling agent to the dampening solution.

Remedy 5: If using compressible blankets, change to quick-release or conventional.

Remedy 6: Change to a higher grade of paper.

**Piling
(halftones)**

Paper coating piles in the middle of halftone printing areas of blankets. After 1,000–2,000 impressions, midtones appear mottled due to slurring, and the blanket appears lumpy in those areas. This happens on the second or subsequent unit(s) of multicolor presses.

Paper coating piling: an enlargement of a print taken at the start of the run *(top)* and the same subject after 2,300 impressions, showing the effects of coating piling in the halftone printing areas

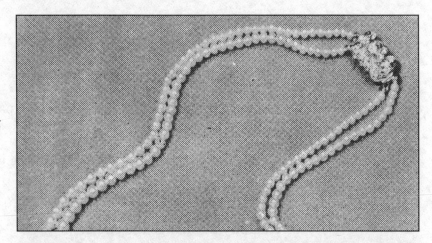

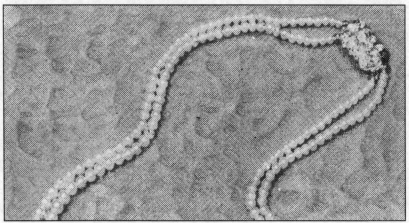

Cause:
The coating adhesive is being softened and rendered tacky by moisture on the first unit; a following unit lifts the adhesive and coating pigment. The removed adhesive and pigment mix with the ink, producing a puttylike combination that sticks to the blanket and builds up to an appreciable thickness.

Remedy 1: Frequently wash the blanket(s) with water and ink solvent to remove the piling.

Remedy 2: Change to a better-sized paper.

Remedy 3: Add isopropyl alcohol (isopropanol) or an alcohol substitute to the dampening solution.

Decreased Paper Gloss

The paper surface has become rough; therefore, gloss is reduced.

Cause A:
Overheating has puffed the groundwood fibers.

Remedy 1: Reduce the web temperature.

Remedy 2: Change to a higher grade of paper.

Cause B:
Overheating has melted the resins in the paper coating.

Remedy 1: Reduce the web temperature.

Remedy 2: Change the paper.

Remedy 3: Add a nonpiling agent to the dampening solution.

Tinting

Overall tint quickly appears on the unprinted areas of coated paper. This tint may appear on the nonimage areas of the plates but can be washed off with water and a sponge.

Cause:
The dampening solution is extracting a surface-active agent from the paper coating, causing the ink to emulsify in the dampening solution on the plate.

Remedy 1: Stiffen the ink as much as possible with a suitable varnish, or run a stiffer ink.

Remedy 2: Change dampening solution, or increase or decrease dampening solution pH and conductivity based on requirements.

Remedy 3: Avoid using any wetting agent in the dampening solution.

Remedy 4: Run another paper.

Yellowing

Paper yellows as it passes through the dryer.

Cause:
The web has been overheated.

Remedy 1: Reduce the dryer heat.

Remedy 2: Increase the press speed.

Remedy 3: Install a pyrometer-controlled circuit on the dryer.

9 Ink Problems

Lithographic ink is a dispersion of a pigment in a fluid vehicle that will print and dry. The pigment provides the color and dictates whether the printed ink film will be transparent or opaque. The vehicle gives the ink fluidity so that it can be distributed by the press inking rollers and applied evenly to the paper. In the printed ink film, the liquid vehicle must be changed to a solid in order to bind the pigment to the printed surface.

Lithographic inks dry by different processes. Ink containing drying oil dries by absorption, oxidation, and polymerization. The vehicle of *quickset* ink is composed of drying oils, resins, and solvents that speed up setting by a process of selective absorption; quickset ink also dries by oxidation and polymerization. Both of these inks are used in web offset printing on newsprint and uncoated papers that are not run through a dryer. *Heatset* inks are dried by evaporation of their solvents with the aid of heat, followed by chilling to solidify the remaining nonvolatile resins in the ink vehicle.

When heatset inks exit the dryer, the printed ink film is in a semifluid state because of its high temperature. Passing the web over the chill rolls sets the ink so that it will not smear, smudge, or set off during finishing operations. The ink may retain some solvent, which eventually evaporates or penetrates the paper.

Heatset ink vehicle primarily consists of resins dissolved in a volatile solvent that boils between 450–600°F (230–315°C). The dryer heats the web and evaporates the solvent, leaving the resin in the ink to bind the pigment to the paper. Webs printed on common-impression-cylinder (CIC) presses must pass through the dryer twice, since only one side of the web is printed at a time.

Heatset inks may be modified by adding drying oils and drier to increase rub- and scuff-resistance; however, excessive modification may cause the inks to remain tacky after drying and chilling.

All lithographic inks except those for waterless offset must work with water. Dampening solution always mixes to some extent with the ink during printing; however, the ink must not waterlog and become pasty. Furthermore, the ink should not break down and emulsify in the dampening solution. If this occurs, nonimage areas of the paper will be printed with a tint of the ink. The inkmaker formulates the ink to meet the requirements of the lithographic process.

The ink film thickness printed by offset lithography is relatively thin compared to other processes; therefore, inks must be more highly pigmented.

Waterless inks. Waterless offset inks contain many of the same ingredients that conventional lithographic inks contain. The difference between them is that waterless inks have vehicles that allow them to have higher initial viscosities than those of the conventional inks. Waterless offset inks also may have slightly lower tacks than those of conventional offset inks. The viscosity and tack differences between the two inks have to do with the differences between the two plates. Conventional offset lithographic plates operate on the principle that oil and water do not mix. They have a hydrophilic nonimage area that attracts water or dampening solution and an oleophilic image area that repels water and attracts oily ink. Waterless offset plates use a silicone material for nonimage areas of the plate. This silicone material has a low surface energy that resists ink if the ink's viscosity is high enough for it to be more attracted to itself than to the silicone material.

The viscosity of a liquid changes rapidly with the temperature. In conventional lithography, the presence of water in the dampening solution on press cools the ink and helps it to maintain a viscosity that does not compromise its physical characteristics while it is being worked. The viscosity of waterless offset inks is maintained on press by a press temperature control system, either a plate cylinder cooling system or an ink oscillator (vibrator) cooling system. Waterless offset inks are formulated at varied viscosities in order to be adaptable to the geographic temperature environment of any press.

When printing by waterless offset, zone controls for each printing unit helps to extend the run length and reduces the printing problems that will occur from one ink color to another color because of the requirements necessary for certain inks to run cooler and certain inks to run warmer.

Ink drying systems. In addition to heatset dryers, which are discussed in chapter 10, "Dryer and Chill Roll Problems," two alternative drying systems are used in web offset.

The ultraviolet (UV) ink drying system involves specially formulated inks and special equipment. When UV inks are exposed to ultraviolet radiation, polymerization occurs almost instantaneously. These inks contain no solvent, so solvent-fume emissions from the press is eliminated. A series of lamps emit UV radiation to cure the ink.

Electron beam (EB) inks are similar to UV inks, except that they do not require photoinitiators. The source for the polymerization is a stream of electrons that bombard the ink film. EB inks have all the advantages of UV inks; they cure rapidly, dry hard, and present no emission control problems. Because they lack photoinitiators, these inks are more stable and more easily handled.

Solving ink-related problems. Because of the many variables involved in inkmaking and lithographic printing, the web offset press operator is constantly faced with situations that require knowledge, experience, and judgment.

Experience and judgment come with practice. The inkmaker is a key source of information when troubleshooting. Usually, it is ill-advised to alter inks, because uniformity is essential for the duration of the pressrun. The complexity of heatset ink formulas presents potential danger if they are altered improperly.

The following section lists the most common ink problems, their probable causes, and remedies to overcome or avoid each problem. Some remedies may not be applicable under certain conditions. For example, the press may not be equipped with the devices that are recommended to remedy a specific problem.

Some chronic ink problems can only be overcome by equipment, which may not be available on press. Management should consider acquiring the equipment required to enhance the productivity of the press.

Changing the paper or ink may not be feasible when the problem arises. Once paper or ink problems are diagnosed, the manufacturer or supplier should be contacted immediately thereafter.

Setoff

Printed ink transfers to an adjacent sheet in the delivery. Ink may also set off during folding and finishing operations.

Cause A:
Dryer temperature is too low relative to the press speed, and the ink solvent is not evaporating completely.

Remedy 1: Raise the dryer temperature, or reduce the press speed.

Remedy 2: Consult the inkmaker about the use of a more volatile solvent.

Cause B:
Ink dries too slowly.

Remedy 1: Increase the dryer temperature.

Remedy 2: Reduce the press speed.

Remedy 3: Have the ink reformulated.

Remedy 4: Change to a more suitable ink.

Cause C:
Chill system is inadequate. Ink resins are not setting hard enough.

Remedy 1: Lower the chill water temperature. Web temperature should not exceed 75°F (24°C) coming off the last chill roll.

Remedy 2: Reduce press speed and dryer temperature.

Remedy 3: Increase the flow rate of the water through the chill rolls if the outlet temperature is too high.

Remedy 4: Increase the wrap of the web around the chill rolls.

Remedy 5: Install additional chill rolls.

Cause D:
Inadequate ventilation of solvent vapors, which cling to the web as it leaves the dryer.

Remedy 1: Increase the velocity of air coming from the air knife at the dryer exit.

Remedy 2: Install an air knife if the press is not so equipped.

Cause E:
Excessive ink film thickness.

Remedy 1: Run less ink.

Remedy 2: Use an ink with more color strength.

Cause F:
Ink contains too much drying oil. (Specialty heatset inks are sometimes formulated with drying oil.)

Remedy: Have the ink reformulated.

Cause G:
Former board and angle bars heat up due to friction and hot compressed air. This heat reduces the cooling effect of the chill rolls.

Remedy: Install a water-cooled system between the compressor and the press. Compressed air should be approximately 60°F (16°C).

Smudging   Dried heatset ink is not rub-resistant.

Cause A:
Ink does not dry and set after passing through the dryer and chill roll sections.

Remedy 1: Increase the dryer temperature.

Remedy 2: Decrease the press speed.

Remedy 3: Have the ink reformulated to better resist rubbing and scuffing.

Cause B:
Dampening solution is too acidic for a specialty ink containing drying oil.

Remedy: Maintain the dampening solution pH and conductivity within the manufacturer's recommendations.

Chalking

Chalking occurs when the dried printed ink film can be rubbed off, exposing the paper surface.

Cause A:
Excessive dryer temperature causes the paper to absorb too much of the ink vehicle, leaving the pigment with insufficient binder.

Remedy: Lower the dryer temperature.

Cause B:
Poor pigment wetting by the vehicle oils.

Remedy: Consult ink supplier.

**Picking/
Splitting**

Picking and splitting are destructive processes by which areas of the paper's surface are separated from the base stock. They may be attributed to excessively tacky ink, inadequately pick-resistant paper, or both.

Cause A:
The force required to split the printed ink film exceeds the surface or internal bond strength of the paper.

Remedy 1: Have the ink reformulated.

Remedy 2: Change to a more pick-resistant paper.

Remedy 3: Increase dampening solution feed to reduce ink tack.

Remedy 4: Increase the ink film thickness. Thin ink films require more force to split.

Picking at the tail
edge of a solid

Remedy 5: Heat the ink and/or dampening solution to reduce ink tack.

Remedy 6: Reduce the press speed.

Cause B:
Heatset ink solvent evaporates during the pressrun, and ink becomes more tacky. Evaporation is also accelerated by heat in the inking system, which is generated by the running press.

Remedy 1: Use an ink with a slower solvent-evaporation rate.

Remedy 2: Cool the ink oscillators by circulating water through them, or chill the ink fountain by refrigeration.

Remedy 3: Chill the dampening solution.

Cause C:
The extra energy required to split a thin ink film accelerates solvent evaporation.

Remedy: Reduce the ink's color strength and increase the ink film thickness.

Cause D:
Ink fed to a light form requires more time to work through the inking system; this allows more time for the solvent to evaporate.

Remedy: Use a solvent with a higher boiling point.

Cause E:
Intermittent stops during the start-up allow time for the solvent to evaporate, thus increasing ink tack.

Remedy 1: During makeready, use *start-up inks* that contain little or no volatile solvents.

Remedy 2: Soften the press ink to counteract stiffening that occurs as solvent evaporates during makeready.

Remedy 3: Spray the ink rollers with heatset oil to keep the ink from drying.

Backing Away   Ink backs away from the fountain roller.

Cause:
The ink sets up in the fountain and no longer flows; therefore, it is not picked up by the fountain roller and transferred into the inking system.

Remedy 1: Install an ink fountain agitator.

Remedy 2: Manually work the ink to keep it fluid.

Remedy 3: Use an ink with a lower yield value.

Piling   Ink piles or cakes on the rollers, plates, or blankets.

Cause A:
Ink accumulates and dries on the rollers, plates, or blankets beyond the edges of the web.

Remedy 1: Reduce ink flow.

Remedy 2: Use an ink with higher color strength, which requires reduced ink feed.

Cause B:
Ink that is too short, waterlogged, or poorly ground piles on the printing areas of the plates and blankets.

Remedy 1: Reduce the dampening to a minimum.

Remedy 2: Have the ink reground or reformulated.

Cause C:
Coating from coated stock is picked up by the blanket, mixed with the ink, and deposited in halftone areas.

Remedy 1: Use a paper that does not cause this problem.

Remedy 2: Add isopropyl alcohol to the dampening solution.

Remedy 3: Add a wetting agent that will permit the use of less dampening solution.

Remedy 4: Use less alcohol substitute in the dampening solution.

Cause D:
New rollers or blankets that have yet to become saturated with ink vehicle or solvent absorb excessive amounts of vehicle and solvent; therefore, ink pigment is retained on the surfaces of the rollers and blankets.

Remedy: Apply a compound that decreases solvent penetration into rollers and blankets. The compound should not affect drying.

Scumming

Ink causes the printing plate to scum. Scum is usually visible on the plate and cannot be removed with a wet sponge. Remove light scum by re-etching the plate.

Cause A:
Printing excessive ink in halftones or printing with ink that is too soft causes the ink to spread into nonimage areas, gradually sensitizing them.

Remedy: Run a stiff, thin ink film.

Cause B:
Abrasive pigment particles or aggregates in the ink gradually wear the plate at the margins of its image areas, causing dots and lines to thicken. Detect pigment particles or aggregates using a Fineness-of-Grind Gauge or Grindometer.

Remedy 1: Have the ink reground.

Remedy 2: Replace the ink.

Cause C:
Ink that is too greasy does not pick up enough water.

Remedy: Replace the ink.

Cause D:
The ink's water pickup is too high, removing an excessive amount of dampening solution from the plate.

Remedy: Consult with ink supplier to select a compatible ink.

Tinting

A tint of ink appears in nonimage areas. The tint is visible on the printed sheets but not necessarily on the plate. The tint may be washed from the plate; however, it recurs when printing is resumed.

Tint of cyan ink in nonimage area

Cause:
The ink insufficiently resists water and emulsifies in the dampening solution.

Remedy 1: Replace the ink.

Remedy 2: Reduce the acid content or alcohol substitute of the dampening solution; reformulate the solution as needed.

NOTE: Low-tack inks designed for use on high-speed presses break down and tint when run on small, low-speed presses.

Poor Trapping

Poor trapping occurs when a wet printed ink film does not adhere or transfer properly to a previously printed wet or dry ink film.

Poor wet trapping of yellow over magenta

Cause A:
Excessive ink tack, relative to the previously printed ink.

Remedy 1: Apply inks with successively decreasing tacks for multicolor presswork.

Remedy 2: Use inks that contain gellants.

Remedy 3: Reduce tack of the ink that fails to trap properly.

Inkometer for measuring the tack of ink

Trapping

Most multicolor web offset printing involves wet trapping of inks, or the printing of ink films over wet ink films to produce intermediate colors. Whether or not the desired colors are produced depends on either the relative thickness of the ink film or the actual amount of ink transferred.

Theoretically, in order to trap or transfer properly, each successive ink should be of lower tack than the previously applied ink film. Practically, this rule applies to printing on nonabsorbent surfaces such as laminated foils and plastics. On absorbent papers, ink films can increase considerably in tack between printing units by setting, so the tack of successively applied inks may be insignificant. The important consideration is the relative tack of two ink films at the instant of printing. If the first-down ink is run spare, the second-down ink may trap even though it has higher tack (as measured out of the can). If the second-down ink is strong and must be run spare, it may not trap on the first-down ink if the first-down ink was run full. However, if a third color is superimposed on the first two, the third-down ink should be less tacky than the first two. Setting of the second-down ink, with its resultant tack increase, is greatly retarded by the first-down ink—even on absorbent stock. As a result, knowledge of ink tacks, color strengths, and the absorbency of paper is essential in avoiding trapping problems.

Gelled varnishes enhance ink trapping. Additional gellant increases thixotropy; inks stiffen quickly when not being worked. Such inks require fountain agitators. However, inks flow through the system readily because they are being worked by the action of the rollers, the plate, and the blanket. Once these inks are printed, they set rather rapidly and provide a stable base for subsequently printed ink films. Back-trapping and dot distortion are reduced, and highlight and shadow dots reproduce more accurately. The stiffness of gelled inks makes them more difficult to load or pump into the ink fountain.

The accuracy of colors produced by wet-trapping solids on solids is affected by changes in gloss. The appearance of the overprinted inks is determined by trapping and gloss, or apparent trapping, which is most accurately measured by a reflection densitometer. Determine trapping performance by printing control patches of each ink as a single ink film and by overprinting pairs of colors. GATF color control bars (e.g., Mini Control Bar for Web, the GATF/SWOP Production Control Bar, and GATF's digital web color control bar package) are designed for this purpose. From densitometer measurements of the patches, it is possible to calculate and control the degree of trapping.

When halftones are printed over solids or other halftones, dot gain can affect the resultant color. Some dot gain is unavoidable in production printing; prepress and platemaking procedures that compensate for anticipated dot gain ultimately produce printed dots of the desired size. The GATF Plate Control Target allows for such control.

The press operator controls dot gain by regulating ink film thickness, properly setting the form rollers, and controlling cylinder pressures—plate-to-blanket and blanket-to-paper. Multicolor tints and halftones should trap properly if the solid overprints of the GATF color control bars are trapping properly.

GATF Digital Four-Color SWOP Production Control Bar, part of the GATF digital web color control bar package (order no. 7321-M, 7321-I)

Remedy 4: Reduce the color strength of the ink that fails to trap properly and run a thicker ink film.

Cause B:
Inks improperly balanced, relative to color strength. A thin ink film does not trap on a previously applied thicker ink film.

Remedy 1: Use inks with proper color strength sequence.

Remedy 2: Print a thin ink film on the first unit.

Remedy 3: Reduce the color strength and increase the ink film thickness of the ink that does not trap properly.

Cause C:
Increased tack due to solvent evaporation by heat generated in the oscillators and rollers. This is aggravated if the web is preheated but not chilled at the infeed.

Remedy 1: Water-cool the oscillators to regulate their temperature.

Remedy 2: Reduce the color strength and increase the ink film thickness of the ink that fails to trap.

Remedy 3: Add heatset oil to reduce the tack of overprinting inks that fail to trap. This procedure inhibits overheating of the printing unit and compensates for solvent evaporation.

Poor Trapping (halftones)

Halftones show poor trapping, dot gain, and improper color, although solids trap properly.

Cause:
Improper ink/water balance.

Remedy 1: Print a thinner ink film by decreasing ink feed, and reduce the dampening solution to the minimum required to keep the nonimage areas of the plate clean.

Remedy 2: Use ink that is compatible with the dampening solution.

Remedy 3: Reduce the amount of dampening solution fed to the plate.

Remedy 4: Add isopropyl alcohol or an alcohol substitute to the dampening solution.

Color Change   The printing changes color during the run, with no changes in inks or paper.

Cause A:
Increasing temperature of the inking system as the run progresses. This evaporates the solvent, thus increasing the ink tack.

Remedy 1: Water-cool the ink oscillators.

Remedy 2: Reduce the tack of the ink that does not trap properly.

Cause B:
Daily or seasonal temperature changes in the pressroom.

Remedy 1: Water-cool the ink oscillators to regulate their temperature.

Remedy 2: Print inks with higher tack and more body as the pressroom temperature increases.

Cause C:
Ink backs away from the fountain roller.

Remedy 1: Install an ink agitator.

Remedy 2: Fill the ink fountain more frequently.

Mottle   Mottle is a printing defect characterized by spotted solids consisting of unevenly transferred ink or uneven ink absorption.

Cause A:
Uncoated stock has wild formation and nonuniform ink absorbency, which can be verified by the K & N Ink Absorbency Test or a flexible-blade ink-wipe test. (See GATF publications *What the Printer Should Know about Ink* and *What the Printer Should Know about Paper.*)

Remedy 1: Use inks with maximum color strength and minimum penetrating qualities.

Using the K& N Ink Absorbency Test to evaluate the ink absorbency of a paper stock

Remedy 2: Change to a different paper.

Remedy 3: Decrease ink tack and strength; increase ink film thickness.

Cause B:
Running too much ink on a hard stock that is not ink-receptive.

Remedy: Increase the color strength and decrease the ink film thickness.

Cause C:
Excessive printing pressure.

Remedy 1: Reduce the printing pressure.

Remedy 2: Stiffen the ink.

Cause D:
Too much dampening solution reduces ink tack so that the ink tends to squash. Excessive moisture also causes snowflaky solids.

Remedy 1: Run the minimum amount of dampening solution required to keep nonimage areas of the plate clean.

Remedy 2: Make sure that the printing plates are adequately desensitized.

Cause E:
The ink holdout characteristics of coated stock is very high.

Remedy: Consult with ink supplier for an ink that will be compatible.

Mechanical (Starvation) Ghosting

Faint images of prints appear in solids or halftones following the printed image.

Cause A:
A narrow solid ahead of or behind a wider solid is consuming much of the ink on the form rollers; therefore, the ink supply is inadequate to print the adjacent wider solid at full strength. The same result is visible in darker halftones.

Remedy 1: Advise the artist to distribute solids, halftones, and type in the layout. Identify layouts that are likely to produce ghosting.

Remedy 2: Run the minimum dampening solution required to keep the nonimage areas of the plate clean.

Remedy 3: Avoid running thin ink films to produce tints. Run a thicker ink film with less color strength.

Remedy 4: If possible, run opaque inks.

Remedy 5: Install one or two oscillating form rollers to laterally distribute the ink.

Remedy 6: Print the GATF Mechanical Ghosting Form to determine the ghosting characteristics of the press.

Cause B:
The blanket is embossed as a result of ink vehicle absorbed during the previous pressrun.

Remedy: Install a new blanket.

NOTE: Clean an embossed blanket thoroughly with blanket wash and hang it in a dark area. This procedure allows absorbed oil to diffuse through the rubber and may reduce embossing.

GATF Mechanical
Ghosting Form (order
no. 7074/7174),
showing mechanical
ghosting (simulated)

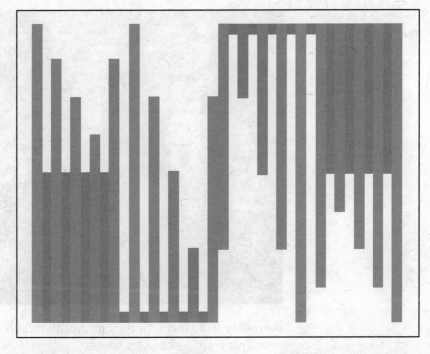

Hickeys

Hickeys are usually doughnut-shaped white spots surrounding a small spot of ink. White spots in solids that are not doughnut-shaped are caused by paper dust or particles. (Review this problem in Chapter 8.)

Cause A:
Hard particles of dried ink or pieces of rubber roller covering.

Remedy 1: Clean the press thoroughly and remove all dried ink from the fountain or on the rollers before inking up the press.

A solid particle (such
as dried ink), enlarged,
on the blanket, pro-
ducing a hickey on
the printed sheet

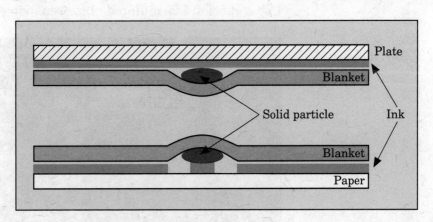

Hickey on a printed
test form

Remedy 2: Lubricate and manually wash roller ends to prevent ink from caking on them.

Remedy 3: Use a hickey-picking roller to remove hickeys from the plate. Clean these rollers regularly.

Cause B:
Flakes of roller composition, usually from glazed or pitted rollers.

Remedy 1: Recondition the form rollers and oscillators to remove the glaze. Glaze is the accumulation of dried ink vehicle and gum not removed by ordinary washup solvents. Use a specially formulated glaze-removing material.

A typical ink-skin
hickey, enlarged

Remedy 2: Use a hickey-picking roller to pick hickeys from the plate. Clean these rollers regularly.

Cause C:
Debris from the ceiling that has fallen into the press.

Remedy 1: Install a new pressroom ceiling.

Remedy 2: Vacuum-clean the ceiling and everything overhead on which dirt can accumulate. Paint the ceiling, or hang plastic sheets over the press to catch falling debris.

Remedy 3: Use a hickey-picking roller to remove hickeys from the plate. Clean these rollers regularly.

Cause D:
Press lacks the ability to minimize hickey problems.

Remedy 1: Install hickey-picking ink form rollers.

Remedy 2: Install a Delta-type dampening system.

Misting

Ink mists or flies, forming fine droplets or filaments that become diffused throughout the pressroom atmosphere. This problem may be attributed to either the ink or the press.

Cause A:
An excessively thick ink film that forms long filaments when split between rollers.

How an ink splits as it emerges from the roller nip and forms flying particles

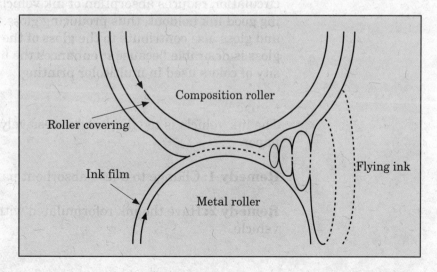

Composition roller

Roller covering

Ink film

Metal roller

Flying ink

Remedy 1: Substitute a more highly pigmented ink, and run a thinner ink film.

Remedy 2: Increase viscosity of ink.

Cause B:
The fountain is feeding too much ink to the fountain roller.

Remedy 1: Tighten the fountain blade to reduce the ink film thickness, and adjust the ratchet to increase roller movement.

Remedy 2: Increase the speed of the ink fountain roller.

Cause C:
The ink is too long and too tacky.

Remedy: Change to a shorter ink with lower tack as recommended by the inkmaker.

Cause D:
Inadequate lateral distribution — too little sideways motion of the oscillators allows ink to form ridges on the rollers and increases its tendency to fly.

Remedy: Increase the oscillation until the ridges disappear.

Dull Print

Printing lacks the desired gloss. One advantage of web offset is its ability to produce glossy printing without the use of anti-setoff sprays. Quick evaporation of the solvent by heat and air circulation reduces absorption of ink vehicle by the paper, giving good ink holdout, thus producing gloss. Paper smoothness and gloss also contribute to the gloss of the printing. High gloss is desirable because it enhances the brilliance and intensity of colors used in multicolor printing.

Cause A:
The ink vehicle is too fluid and excessively penetrates the paper.

Remedy 1: Change to a less-absorbent paper.

Remedy 2: Have the ink reformulated with a less-penetrating vehicle.

Cause B:
The paper is too absorbent.

Remedy 1: Run a compatible ink.

Remedy 2: Change to a less-absorbent or coated paper with higher ink holdout.

Cause C:
Extreme dryer heat makes the resin binder too fluid and penetrating, reducing gloss.

Remedy 1: Reduce the dryer temperature and/or increase the press speed.

Remedy 2: Reformulate the ink with a more volatile solvent, thus enabling the dryer temperature to be reduced.

Cause D:
Running with too much dampening solution. Excessive moisture in the ink prevents the transfer of a smooth ink film required for high gloss.

Remedy: Reduce the dampening solution to the minimum required to keep the nonimage areas of the plate clean.

Cause E:
Excessive dryer heat causes fiber puffing or roughening of the paper surface.

Remedy 1: Reduce the dryer temperature and/or increase the web speed.

Remedy 2: Use a higher grade of paper.

Dot Gain

Printed halftones show excessively higher dot sizes than the plate images.

Cause A:
Too much form roller-to-plate, plate-to-blanket, or blanket-to-blanket pressures.

Remedy: Check and correct roller settings as needed.

Cause B:
The ink is too long and squashes under printing pressure.

Remedy: Print a stiffer, shorter ink.

Cause C:
Halftone dots are slurred or doubled.

Remedy: See the following problems in Chapter 3: "Doubling" and "Slurring."

Cause D:
The plate was not exposed and processed to manufacturer's specifications to compensate for dot gain on press.

Remedy: Coordinate film making and platemaking procedures to obtain sharper halftone negatives, positives, and plates that allow for dot gain on press. Use the GATF Dot Gain Scale-II or GATF Plate Control Target on plates to monitor and control dot sizes.

Dot gain, which could be caused by excessive inking or incorrect plate exposure

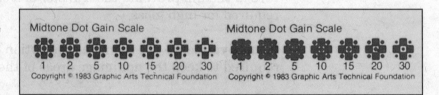

Cause E:
Color separations do not properly compensate for dot gain on press.

Remedy: Use a GATF press test form and conduct a press optimization process to determine proper dot gain compensation when making color separations.

10   Dryer and Chill Roll Problems

Dryers

Heatset inks currently dominate the commercial web offset field. Web offset forms printing and newspaper work, on the other hand, chiefly rely on quickset and absorptive inks that do not require drying and chilling capacity built into the press. The need for a dryer and chill rolls depends on the ink used and how its dries.

Quickset inks (including web offset newspaper inks) dry chiefly by penetration. This drying process leaves the print with a dull, flat finish. Other quickset inks oxidize after the solvent-absorption phase. Their use is restricted by the need for highly absorbent papers.

Heatset inks dry with high gloss and are compatible with nearly all stocks. Their formulation is as complex as that found in any ink. Drying equipment is required on the press to evaporate volatile solvent. Chill rolls cool the heat-softened binding resins. The solvent reduces the ink's viscosity, leaving solid pigment particles embedded in semisoft resins. Final solidification or setting occurs with the cooling of the binding resins. Final drying occurs off the press and consists of an oxidation process several hours to several days long.

The solvent evaporates quickly and violently; air temperature in the dryer may reach 500°F (260°C). The average time the web spends in the dryer is only about 0.7 sec., but it exits with a surface temperature of up to 300°F (149°C). Less than a second later, the chill rolls cool the web to about 75°F (24°C).

All blanket-to-blanket presses employ floating dryers, because the web has ink on both sides. Floating dryers are classed according to the method used to heat the web. The oldest design is the **open flame,** or **direct-impingement, dryer.**

High-velocity hot-air dryers. High-velocity hot-air dryers, the most common design today, blow hot air at the web. Alternately spaced nozzles put a controlled ripple in the web to prevent it from wrinkling or corrugating in the dryer. Between the nozzles are exhaust ducts that vent solvent-laden air and help to maintain air circulation in the dryer. The mixture of hot air and ink solvent vapor is then recirculated through the combustion chamber, which burns much of the solvent.

Combination dryers. Combination dryers use both the open-flame and medium-velocity hot-air techniques. The first half of the dryer usually contains the flame nozzles, and the second half the hot-air section.

The high-velocity hot-air dryer has one important advantage over the flame dryer. Next to the moving web is a thin layer of air that moves with the web, a boundary layer that is part of the moving web's aerodynamics. When solvents are evaporated, they accumulate in this boundary layer until it is saturated. Once the air is saturated, more heat is needed to continue solvent evaporation. This lowers dryer efficiency. In a high-velocity hot-air dryer, therefore, turbulence is introduced into the boundary layer to prevent saturation.

Chill Rolls

The chill stand is an assembly of driven steel drums positioned after the dryer. They are cooled by refrigerated water circulating through them. Most chill stands are designed with three or more rolls.

Most chill rolls are driven by the press drive through a variable-speed transmission. The speed of the chill rolls is adjustable over a fairly wide range. With this variable-speed control, the chill rolls regulate web tension in the long span from the last printing unit through the dryer.

Water circulation in the chill rolls should be through a closed system. This minimizes mineral deposits inside the chill rolls, which can impair chilling efficiency. In addition, chill roll monitors should measure temperature at the outlet of the roll rather than at the water inlet. Outlet temperatures are adjusted to differences in web temperature after the web leaves the dryer.

The time that the paper spends in the dryer must coincide with press speed and dryer length. Higher press speed reduces the time for the heat to release the solvent. With a short dryer, press speed must be slowed to adequately dry the web.

The dryer should be set to the *minimum* temperature required to burn off the ink solvent. When the paper is chilled, folded, and delivered, it should not mark, smear, or set off. Minimum heat lessens the chance of blistering, reduces moisture loss, and, in many cases, improves printed ink gloss.

To determine minimum dryer temperature, set press speed at the desired rate and the dryer at a *safe* temperature — neither too high nor too low. Web temperature after chilling should be 75°F (24°C) or less.

Never raise the dryer temperature without first making sure that the web is being adequately chilled. When press speed or dryer temperature is increased thereafter, always make sure that the web temperature after chilling is no higher than 75°F (24°C).

Chill Roll Plumbing

The illustration on the next page shows several different methods for plumbing three- and four-roll chill systems. At the top of the illustration are drawings that show the physical layout of the chill rolls. It should be noted that the roller markings A, B, and C (and for the four-roll system, D) do not represent the physical location of the rollers but rather the sequence in which the web out of the dryer runs over the various rollers. For clarity, in the four systems marked I, II, III, and IV, the rollers are shown from left to right in the order in which the web contacts them.

Table A shows the flow rate in gallons per minute or liters per minute through each chill roll for the various systems illustrated. These rates assume a total water supply of 25 gal./min. (95 l/min.). In the case of diagram IV, it is further assumed that it is possible to pump the entire water supply through all of the chill rolls hooked in series.

Table A:
Flow rate per chill roll in gallons (liters) per minute with a 25-gpm (95-lpm) supply

Diagram	Three-Roll System		Four-Roll System	
I	8.3 gpm	31.4 lpm	6.2 gpm	23.5 lpm
II	8.3	31.4	6.2	23.5
III	12.5	47	12.5	47
IV	25	95	25	95

For the purpose of the calculations, it is assumed that the paper coming out of the dryer is at a temperature of 270°F (132°C), paper temperature off of the last chill roll is 75°F (24°C), the chill rolls in the three-roll system are large enough to provide the same amount of surface contact with

Chill roll plumbing

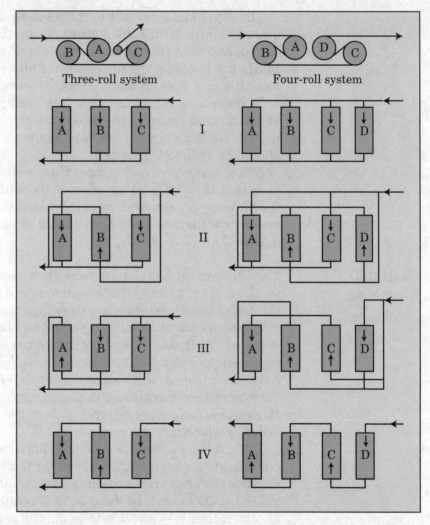

the web as that for the four-roll system, and the temperature of the water being supplied to the chill system is 55°F (13°C).

For both three- and four-roll systems (Table B), plumbing diagrams III and IV provide slightly better cooling because of the increased velocity of the water running through the individual chill rolls. The four-roll system illustrated by diagram III works nearly as well as diagram IV, although the flow

Table B:
Average web
temperature after
chilling

Diagram	Three-Roll System		Four-Roll System	
I	76.5°F	24.7°C	76.6°F	24.8°C
II	76.5	24.7	76.6	24.8
III	75.6	24.2	75.3	24.1
IV	75.0	23.9	75.0	23.9

rate of water through the chill rolls is only 12.5 gal./min. (47 l/min.) for diagram III as opposed to 25 gal./min. (95 l/min.) for diagram IV.

Table C shows the side-to-side web temperature variations in the web after chilling. The temperature variations for diagram I are significantly larger than those for diagrams II, III, and IV. The problem with diagram I for either a three- or four-roll system is that because of the plumbing method, all of the chill rolls are cold on the same side of the press and relatively warm on the opposite side of the press. With diagrams II, III, and IV, the cold water input is alternated from side to side as the web goes across the chill rolls. If it is necessary to lower the web temperature to 75°F (24°C) in order to avoid marking in the folder, the 8°F (4°C) side-to-side temperature differential produced by plumbing as indicated in diagram I will mean that the cold side of the web must be chilled to 67°F (19°C) in order for the warm side to be down to 75°F (24°C). This extra cooling requirement limits press production speeds.

Table C:
Side-to-side temperature variation after chilling

Diagram	Three-Roll System		Four-Roll System	
I	8.1°F	4.5°C	8.0°F	4.4°C
II	2.7	1.5	0.1	0.1
III	2.0	1.1	0.0	0.0
IV	0.9	0.5	0.0	0.0

The chill rolls are plumbed from the last to the first. Chill roll temperatures should decrease successively from the first roll that the web touches to the last. This arrangement prevents surface-only setting. Furthermore, the first roll should reduce the web temperature by 50%; the remaining rolls should lower the web to room temperature.

Drying heatset inks removes moisture from the web. The amount of moisture remaining depends upon several variables: the ink, amount of ink coverage, the paper, and the dryer. The moisture content of the dried web has been reduced below a satisfactory level; therefore, remoisturizing is generally required. Remoisturizing improves dimensional stability, reduces static electricity, and enhances subsequent binding and finishing operations.

There are several remoisturizing systems on the market. These systems range from direct sprays to brush sprays to roller applicators. Silicone applicators are used on the underside of the web to prevent marking in the folder; however, both sides of the web should be remoisturized whenever heat is used as the drying medium.

Solving Dryer and Chill Roll Problems

The following section lists the most common dryer and chill roll problems, their probable causes, and remedies to overcome or avoid each problem. Some remedies may not be applicable under certain conditions. For example, the press may not be equipped with the devices that are recommended to remedy a specific problem.

Management should consider acquiring the equipment required to enhance the productivity of the press. If the remedy suggests a major repair, management should schedule the repair.

Changing the paper or ink may not be feasible when the problem arises. Once paper or ink problems are diagnosed, the manufacturer or supplier should be contacted immediately thereafter.

Uneven Ink Drying

Cause:
Plate dampening is uneven or erratic.

Remedy: Keep dampener covers clean and free from accumulated ink.

Wet Ink

Ink fails to dry, marks on the chill rolls, and smears in the delivery.

Cause A:
The dryer temperature is too low to drive off ink solvent vapors.

Remedy 1: Raise the dryer temperature.

Remedy 2: Reduce the press speed.

Remedy 3: Increase the air velocity in the dryer to cut through and remove the thin air and vapor layer that clings to the moving web.

Cause B:
Dryer is too short or improperly engineered for the press speed or the work being printed.

Remedy 1: Reduce the press speed.

Remedy 2: Replace the dryer.

Cause C:
Inadequate chill capacity to reduce the web temperature to 75°F (24°C).

Remedy 1: Reduce the temperature of the cooling water.

Remedy 2: Increase the circulation of the cooling water.

Remedy 3: Reduce the press speed and dryer temperature.

Remedy 4: Install additional chill rolls.

Cause D:
Reduced water flow in chill rolls due to mineral buildup on the inside of the rolls and plumbing.

Remedy: Reverse-flush rollers and plumbing with acid solution. Consult the chill roll manufacturer.

Cause E:
Running heavy paper, heavy ink coverage, or both.

Remedy 1: Raise the dryer temperature.

Remedy 2: Reduce the press speed.

Remedy 3: Increase the air velocity in the dryer.

Remedy 4: Change to a faster drying ink containing solvents that have a lower boiling point or resins that more readily yield ink solvent. A limit is reached when the inks dry and "tack up" in the printing units. Tackiness, however, can be minimized by water-cooling the ink oscillators. When changing inks, consult the inkmaker.

Remedy 5: Install additional chill rolls.

Cause F:
The temperature of the web leaving the dryer is not uniform from side to side. This can be checked by running an unprinted

web through the dryer. The heat of the web can be measured with a hand-held thermocouple or infrared pyrometer.

Remedy: Clean air knives or scavengers to ensure that hot air flows evenly across the web width.

Setoff   Ink sets off in the folder or delivery.

Cause A:
The ink has surface-dried only. After chilling, the ink solvent works toward and softens the surface, causing setoff. This is most likely to occur when printing heavy ink coverage on hard, nonabsorbent papers.

Remedy 1: Reduce the press speed. If the slower web overheats, reduce the dryer temperature. Maximum web temperature should not exceed 350°F (177°C).

Remedy 2: Install a water-cooled system between the air compressor and the former board and angle bars. Refrigerate the compressed air to 60°F (16°C).

Cause B:
Ink is still tacky after it leaves the chill rolls. Chill rolls are not cooling the printed web enough to harden and set the resin ink binder.

Remedy 1: Increase the circulation of the cooling water, lower its temperature, or both.

Remedy 2: Install an evaporative cooler or refrigerating unit to supply colder water.

Remedy 3: Check the water temperature at the chill roll outlets. If the water is cool enough but the web temperature is too high, the chill rolls may have mineral deposits accumulated on the insides. Remove the deposits by flushing out the rolls. Install a recirculating system.

Remedy 4: If the water temperature is cold enough but the web temperature is too high, the chill rolls may have insufficient surface area. Increase the number of chill rolls, or rearrange the existing chill rolls so that the moving web contacts as much of each chill roll's surface as possible.

Remedy 5: If ink sets properly on one edge of the web but remains tacky on the other, there is probably a temperature gradient across the chill rolls. In this case, change the plumbing to the chill rolls to create a more efficient chill system. Refer to the beginning of this chapter.

Hue Change

The ink changes in hue or loses brightness on passing through the dryer.

Cause A:
Heat resistance of ink pigments is too low for the dryer temperature. Reds are the most susceptible to change.

Remedy 1: Reduce the dryer temperature and the press speed.

Remedy 2: Use inks with more heat-resistant pigments.

Cause B:
Excessive heat in the dryer causes the ink vehicle resin to excessively penetrate the paper, thus reducing gloss. Ink is overdried.

Remedy 1: Reduce the dryer temperature.

Remedy 2: Increase the press speed if the chilling capacity is insufficient.

Cause C:
Paper is too absorbent for the ink. The ink may excessively penetrate the paper, even before entering the dryer.

Remedy 1: Have the ink reformulated.

Remedy 2: Change to a less-absorbent paper.

Reduced Gloss

Ink gloss is lost or reduced in the dryer.

Cause:
Excessive ink-vehicle penetration into the web.

Remedy 1: Reduce the dryer heat, thus reducing the web temperature.

Remedy 2: Increase the press speed to reduce the web temperature if the chilling capacity is insufficient.

Remedy 3: Print inks with better holdout.

Remedy 4: Use higher-viscosity inks.

Blistering

Coated paper blisters as it passes through the dryer. Blisters occurring in the dryer are nearly round, have sharp edges, and appear on both sides of the sheet. They are most commonly found in printed solids, especially those that are backed up with solids. Blisters never occur on uncoated paper.

Cause A:
Excessive moisture content in the web. The high dryer heat vaporizes the moisture, which cannot escape fast enough; therefore, it ruptures the interior of the paper.

Blisters caused by rapid heating, excess moisture, or heavy ink coverage

Remedy 1: Order paper with lower moisture content.

Remedy 2: Install a preheater in the press infeed to reduce and even out the moisture content.

Remedy 3: Reduce the press speed and the dryer temperature. This slows the moisture vaporization and thereby permits the moisture to escape through the pores of the coating without rupturing it.

Remedy 4: Increase the speed of the press without changing the dryer temperature.

Remedy 5: In a multizone dryer, lower the temperature in the first zone; increase the temperature in the second and/or third zone if necessary.

Remedy 6: Use paper with a more porous coating. Double-coated or blade-coated papers are the most susceptible to blistering.

Cause B:
Printing of heavyweight coated stock. At 4% moisture content, an 80-lb. book paper contains twice as much moisture per square inch as does 40-lb. book paper. Therefore, twice as much moisture must escape at drying temperature.

Remedy: Run heavy stock at reduced press speed, and lower the dryer temperature. Heavy webs require longer dryers and additional chill rolls.

Cause C:
Printing solids with thick ink films, especially back-to-back. Ink fills the pores of the coating and slows the escape of water vapor. Blistering typically occurs in heavily printed solids, rather than in halftones or nonimage areas.

Remedy 1: Run thinner ink films of more highly pigmented inks to minimize pore blockage. This may lower the gloss but should minimize the blockage.

Remedy 2: Try remedies listed under "Blistering," Cause A.

11 Delivery Problems

Web offset presses deliver paper in many different forms. Most presses are equipped with a folder, of which there are several designs. Folders are designed for specific jobs; however, they vary in the page size that they can handle and the number of folds that they can execute. Auxiliary equipment may be added to perform imprinting, numbering, punching, perforating, interleaving, gluing, and bundling. Each of these operations generates specific problems under certain conditions. This chapter lists problems that may be attributed to paper and ink and the printing, drying, and chilling operations.

Some presses are equipped with a sheeter and a folder. In such cases, the web must be remoisturized to remove static and enable proper delivery and jogging of the sheets. Remoisturizing helps to prevent cracking when the paper is folded. Remoisturizers should be used on both sides of the web whenever heatset ink drying is part of the printing operation. Remoisturizing improves dimensional stability, reduces static electricity, and enhances subsequent binding and finishing operations.

The following section lists the most common delivery problems, their probable causes, and remedies to overcome or avoid each problem. Some remedies may not be applicable under certain conditions. For example, the press may not be equipped with the devices that are recommended to remedy a specific problem.

Management should consider acquiring the equipment required to enhance the productivity of the press. If the remedy suggests a major repair, management should schedule the repair.

Changing the paper or ink may not be feasible when the problem arises. Once paper or ink problems are diagnosed, the manufacturer or supplier should be contacted immediately thereafter.

Variable Cutoff Misregister

The web sags going into the folder, causing variable cutoff misregister.

Cause A:
Overpacked blankets in the printing unit.

Remedy 1: Check the blanket packing with a packing gauge, and remove as much of the packing as necessary to bring the blankets to the recommended height.

Remedy 2: Check the diameter of the driven rollers feeding the folder. If variable cutoff is a chronic problem, these rollers may be undersized or worn.

Cause B:
Insufficient web tension; the speed of the chill rolls is too high or the folder speed is too low.

Remedy: Increase the speed of the folder, or decrease the speed of the chill rolls until the web is under normal tension.

Gusset Wrinkles

A gusset wrinkle is the crimping of the inside pages of a closed-head signature at the corner where the backbone fold meets the head fold.

Cause:
The outside pages and the inside pages of such a signature are subjected to opposite stresses. The paper is too stiff or

A gusset wrinkle

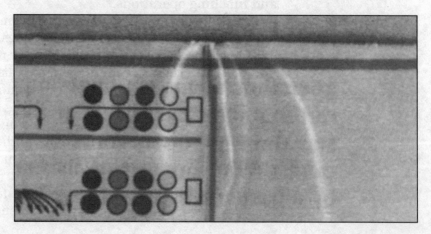

heavy to be folded smoothly into a closed-head signature. The problem is created when the cross fold is made.

Remedy: Perforate along the head to allow the inside and outside sheets to move, relative to each other.

Wrinkling

The web wrinkles as it passes over the former board.

Cause:
The former board is misaligned, relative to the direction of web travel.

Remedy 1: Adjust the angle of the former board.

Remedy 2: Perforate the center of the web prior to running it over the former board.

Cutoff Misregister

Cause:
Poor web tension control.

Remedy 1: Check the roll of paper on the infeed. If it is tapered or shows flats or welts, replace the roll.

Remedy 2: Equip the press with a constant-tension infeed.

Remedy 3: Check for shrinkage in the dryer, which results in the folder overpulling the paper or the web pulling out of the jaws of the jaw folder. Reduce the folder speed or increase the chill roll speed.

Remedy 4: Check electronic cutoff control and adjust for proper operation.

Sidelay Variation

The position of the printed image varies relative to the edges of the web.

Cause A:
Sidelay of the printing is varying because the web is weaving at the infeed. Welts, corrugations, or soft spots may cause the web to weave.

Remedy 1: Check the roll for defects, and replace it if needed.

Remedy 2: Make sure that the festoon rollers of the zero-speed splicer are parallel and level.

Cause B:
Excessive air is blowing through the angle bars of the ribbon folder, causing the webs to stray sideways and be out of register with each other.

Remedy 1: Reduce the air pressure in the angle bars until side-slippage stops.

Remedy 2: Increase tension in the angle bar section.

Poor Folding

Cause A:
The paper has been dehydrated in the dryer, causing roughness and cracking at the fold(s).

Remedy 1: Use remoisturizing equipment to restore the moisture content of the paper.

Remedy 2: Reduce the dryer temperature to the minimum required to dry the ink.

Remedy 3: Score the backbone to lessen the cracking at the fold.

Cause B:
The paper is too bulky and produces bulky signatures.

Remedy 1: Slit the web ahead of the former fold.

Remedy 2: Perforate the web ahead of the former board.

Smudging and Scuffing

The printed ink is smudged or scuffed in the folder section.

Cause A:
Ink has not dried hard enough.

Remedy 1: Make sure that the dryer is adequately hot; preheat the dryer before start-up.

Remedy 2: Raise the dryer temperature, and/or increase the air circulation.

Remedy 3: Reduce the dryer temperature and the press speed if the ink is only surface-dried.

Remedy 4: Acquire a longer dryer, if the problem can be attributed to a dryer that is too short.

Cause B:
The web has not been properly chilled, and the resinous ink binder is still soft. The web temperature should not exceed 75°F (24°C) on leaving the chill rolls.

Remedy 1: Reduce the temperature of the chill rolls. If cooling water temperature is too high, refrigerate the water.

Remedy 2: Plumb the chill rolls to efficiently dissipate the heat of the web.

Remedy 3: Increase the flow rate of the chill water.

Remedy 4: Reduce the press speed and dryer temperature.

Cause C:
Solvent vapors cling to the web as it leaves the dryer; the vapors condense when chilled and soften the dried ink.

Remedy: Install air knives to prevent the layer of solvent vapors from following the web to the chill rolls.

Cause D:
Too much friction at the former nose.

Remedy 1: Reduce the folder speed or increase the chill roll speed to reduce web tension.

Remedy 2: Apply a coating on the former nose to decrease friction. Specific tape is designed for this purpose.

Remedy 3: Install a water-cooled system between the compressor and the press. Refrigerate the air to 60°F (16°C).

Cause E:
Angle bars on the ribbon folder are marking the web, because the bars are set at an incorrect angle.

Remedy 1: Reset angle bars that are misaligned.

Remedy 2: Increase the air pressure of the angle bars.

Remedy 3: Install a water-cooled system between the compressor and the press. Refrigerate the air to 60°F (16°C).

Static

Cause:
The paper is charged with static electricity and fails to deliver and jog properly.

Remedy 1: Lower the dryer temperature. Excessive heat removes too much moisture from the web, thus generating static.

Remedy 2: Check the web temperature as it comes off the chill rolls. If it exceeds 75°F (24°C), increase the flow rate or lower the temperature of the water.

Remedy 3: Remoisturize the paper. The web must be adequately chilled prior to remoisturizing. Add fabric softener to the water in the remoisturizing unit.

Remedy 4: Install antistatic tapes in the sheeter.

Three-roll system for coating or remoisturizing the web
Courtesy Dahlgren USA, Inc.

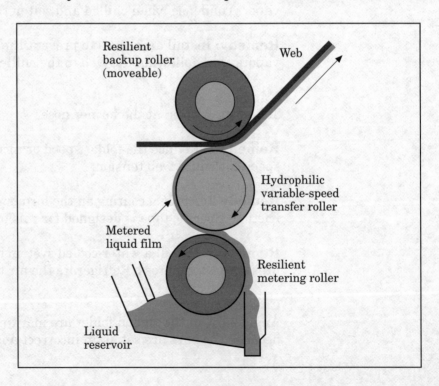

Roll applicator system
to apply moisture to
the web

Curl

Paper curl prevents proper delivery and jogging.

Cause:
Curl is generally due to excessive drying of the paper.

Remedy 1: Lower the dryer temperature.

Remedy 2: Remoisturize the paper.

12 Print Quality Problems

In the early stages of web offset, print quality was poor in comparison to sheetfed offset. As a result of various improvements and the experience gained over the years in practical production, web offset has become established as a quality printing method. Web offset printing is competitive with sheetfed offset and gravure.

The high speed of web offset presses generates excessive waste in a relatively short time; therefore, press operators must know how to operate equipment most efficiently and be able to quickly solve problems when they arise. Electronic press controls for color and register precisely regulate inking and dampening and adjust the position of the plate cylinders and the moving web. The press operator performs these functions from a console, which provides information so that the operator can continuously monitor the pressrun.

Test images are quality control devices that, when printed, allow the press operator to evaluate print quality and press performance. These devices are specifically designed to indicate variations between an original image and the final printed image. Numerous factors contribute to print quality, and many test images may be used singly or in combination to assess press performance or control production.

The following section lists the most common print quality problems, their probable causes, and remedies to overcome or avoid each problem. Some remedies may not be applicable under certain conditions. For example, the press may not be equipped with the devices that are recommended to remedy a specific problem.

Some chronic print quality problems can only be overcome by equipment, which may not be available on press. Management should consider acquiring the equipment required to enhance the productivity of the press. If the remedy suggests a major repair, management should schedule the repair.

Changing the paper or ink may not be feasible when the problem arises. Once paper or ink problems are diagnosed, the manufacturer or supplier should be contacted immediately thereafter.

Misregister (web direction)

Web offset presses have controls for adjusting the position of the printed image. These controls register one color to another and synchronize the cutoff with the printed work.

Circumferential misregister

In this case, the magenta is out of register.

Cause A:
One or more plates are printing longer or shorter images than the others.

Remedy: Transfer packing from the blanket to the plate to shorten the print, or from the plate to blanket to lengthen the print. Maintain tension on the web.

Cause B:
One or more plates are cocked or are not properly registered on the cylinders.

Remedy: Plates must be properly bent on the plate bender. A pneumatically controlled device equipped with register pins ensures consistent, accurate bending. If a manual bending device is used, one person should bend all plates. Two or three people are required to mount larger plates.

A plate bending device

Cause C:
Blankets are packed unevenly. If one printing unit is not pulling the web fast enough, web tension between it and the next unit builds up until the web snaps back, causing misregister.

Remedy: Adjust blanket packing to equalize the draw between the units. All blankets should be packed to the same height from unit to unit.

Cause D:
Web tension is too low.

Remedy: Increase the web tension in the infeed of the press. Install a constant-tension infeed.

Cause E:
Web tension changes during the pressrun due to changing infeed tension.

Remedy: Equip the press with a constant-tension infeed.

Cause F:
Ink tack is too high, causing excessive variations in the wrap of the web on the blankets in areas of solids. These local tension variations produce misregister.

Remedy 1: Use ink with a lower tack value.

Remedy 2: Increase web tension.

Remedy 3: Reduce the press speed.

Remedy 4: Switch to a quick-release blanket.

NOTE: Ink tack can temporarily change during press stops and starts. Water-cooling the ink oscillators minimizes such a change.

Cause G:
Paper coating piles on the blanket.

Remedy 1: Wash the blanket frequently.

Remedy 2: Install automatic blanket washers on the press.

Remedy 3: Change to a more moisture-resistant paper.

Cause H:
Press speed has been changed; web tension was not corrected.

Remedy 1: Adjust web tension until register is obtained.

Remedy 2: Equip the press with a constant-tension infeed.

Remedy 3: Increase the distance between the infeed and the first printing unit.

Cause I:
Out-of-round roll or a roll with flat spots.

Remedy 1: Store paper on end.

Remedy 2: Equip the press with a constant-tension infeed.

Remedy 3: Increase the distance between the infeed and the first printing unit.

Remedy 4: Change to a new roll.

Misregister (lateral)

Side-to-side misregister is more likely to occur with wide webs.

Cause A:
Nonuniform moisture content across the web causes corrugation and misregister.

Remedy 1: Increase the distance between the infeed and the first printing unit.

Remedy 2: Equip the press with a preheater.

Remedy 3: Equip the press with a curved roller to spread and flatten the web.

Cause B:
Moisture welts.

Remedy 1: Do not unwrap rolls until they are to be used.

Remedy 2: Slab off outer layers of paper until the welts are eliminated.

Cause C:
Uneven paper caliper across the web.

Remedy 1: Replace the paper.

Remedy 2: Increase the distance between the infeed and the first printing unit.

Cause D:
Web has slack edges due to moisture pickup.

Remedy 1: Replace the paper.

Remedy 2: Do not unwrap rolls until they are to be used.

Remedy 3: Increase the distance between the infeed and the first printing unit.

Remedy 4: Increase the web tension to tighten slack edges.

Remedy 5: Equip the press with a curved roller to spread and flatten the web.

Lateral misregister

Remedy 6: Adjust the eccentric-mounted infeed roller to balance edge tension.

Cause E:
Ink tack is too high, causing excessive variations in the wrap of the web on the blankets in areas of solids. These local tension variations affect running register, side-to-side register, and cutoff register.

Remedy 1: Reduce the tack of the inks printing the solids.

Remedy 2: Increase web tension.

Remedy 3: Reduce the web speed.

Remedy 4: Switch to a quick-release blanket.

NOTE: Ink tack can temporarily change during press stops and starts. Water-cooling the ink oscillators minimizes such a change.

Fan-out

The first-down color prints wider across the web than later colors.

Cause A:
The tension under which the roll was originally wound exceeds the tension under which it runs through the press; therefore, the paper shortens in the grain direction and widens in the across-the-grain direction.

Remedy 1: Equip the press with bustle wheels, which raise the center of the web and draw in its sides.

Remedy 2: Progressively step out the images on the plates.

Bustle wheels

Remedy 3: Increase the length of the infeed either by running the paper through a festoon or by increasing the distance between the infeed and the first printing unit.

Remedy 4: Increase tension between the printing units.

Cause B:
Moisture applied by the printing units. Although fan-out is not caused by the amount of moisture in the paper, it is aggravated by additional moisture applied by the printing units.

Remedy: Run the minimum amount of dampening solution required to keep the nonimage areas of the plate clean.

Cause C:
Web tension is less between units than at the infeed. The initial stretch of the web, therefore, decreases in the printing section and allows the web width to increase after the first color is printed; succeeding colors print narrow.

Remedy 1: Decrease web tension at the infeed.

Remedy 2: Increase the web tension in the printing section of the press.

Snowflaky Solids

Printing appears snowflaky; solids print nonuniformly.

Cause A:
Ink takes up water. When the ink film is split, water droplets are exposed. These droplets prevent uniform ink transfer to the paper.

Remedy: Reduce the flow of dampening solution. If the ink on the rollers appears to be waterlogged, change to an ink that resists waterlogging.

Cause B:
Rough paper surface, usually uncoated stock.

Remedy 1: Increase the blanket-to-blanket pressure.

Remedy 2: Soften the ink to improve coverage.

Remedy 3: Use compressible blankets.

Dot Gain

Printed images lack sharpness, even with good plates.

Cause A:
Inks are too soft for the press speed. Stiffer inks normally print sharper, especially in halftones.

Remedy 1: Increase press speed.

Remedy 2: Use tackier inks or add gellants to existing inks; consult the inkmaker.

Cause B:
Excessive or nonuniform dampening. Molleton roller covers may be worn or dirty.

Remedy 1: Reduce dampening to the minimum required to keep the nonimage areas of the plate clean.

Remedy 2: Clean or replace dampener roller covers.

Remedy 3: Use paper dampener roller covers.

Cause C:
Slurring or doubling.

Remedy: See Chapter 3, "Printing Unit Problems."

Cause D:
Line and halftone images on the plate are not sharp enough to compensate for normal press gain.

Remedy: Coordinate film making and platemaking activities to produce plates with images that compensate for image gain on press.

Cause E:
Films produced without compensation for dot gain.

Remedy: Use a GATF press test form and conduct a press optimization process to determine proper dot gain compensation when making films.

Dull Print

Printing lacks gloss or finish. One advantage of web offset printing is that antisetoff sprays are not required. Solvents evaporate quickly, which reduces ink vehicle absorption into the paper. High ink holdout produces gloss. The degree of paper smoothness and gloss also affect the appearance of the printed piece.

Cause A:
The ink vehicle is too fluid and/or the paper is too absorbent.

Remedy 1: Obtain a compatible ink.

Remedy 2: Use a less-absorbent paper or paper with a coating designed to give better ink holdout.

Cause B:
A web that is preheated at the infeed warms the press and reduces ink vehicle viscosity, which increases ink penetrating power.

Remedy 1: Reduce the preheater temperature.

Remedy 2: Do not preheat the web.

Remedy 3: Install chill rolls between the preheater and the first printing unit.

Cause C:
Excessive dryer heat liquifies the resin binder, which penetrates the paper and reduces gloss.

Remedy: Reduce the dryer temperature or increase the press speed. Use ink with a volatile solvent that evaporates at a lower temperature.

Cause D:
Excessive dampening solution prevents smooth ink lay and reduces gloss.

Remedy: Reduce the dampening solution to the minimum required to keep the nonimage areas of the plate clean.

Cause E:
The ink is too highly pigmented. The amount of binder remaining on the paper is insufficient to cover all pigment particles.

Remedy: Print a thicker film of a less pigmented ink; consult the inkmaker.

Fiber Puffing

Fiber puffing appears as an overall roughness, usually in the printing areas. This occurs only on paper made from groundwood pulp.

Cause:
The water contained in small clumps of fibers is being changed to water vapor too rapidly and is causing the clumps to burst. This roughens the paper surface.

Remedy 1: Slow the press to reduce thermal shock in the dryer.

Remedy 2: Use paper that contains no groundwood pulp.

Mottle (solids)

Cause:
Heavy paper is linting on press.

Remedy 1: Increase the flow of dampening solution to reduce linting and dusting on the first one or two units.

Remedy 2: Change to a higher grade of paper.

Ink film mottle

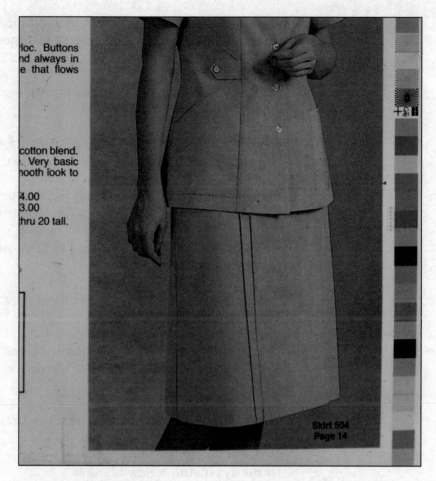

Remedy 3: Reduce the flow of dampening solution on the latter units to prevent the paper from softening if coating or filler is building up on the blankets.

Remedy 4: Add a nonpiling agent to the dampening solution.

Remedy 5: Wash blankets frequently.

Remedy 6: Increase blanket packing 0.002 in. (0.005 mm). Additional pressure helps to scrub accumulations from the blanket.

Ghosting

Ghost images appear in solids or halftones.

Cause A:
A narrow solid ahead of or behind a wider solid consumes much of the ink on the form rollers; therefore, there is not

enough ink to print a full-strength solid in the adjacent areas of the wider solid. The same result is noticeable in darker halftones.

Remedy 1: Whenever possible, multiple solids in a single form should be well-distributed.

Remedy 2: Reduce the dampening solution to the minimum required to keep the nonimage areas clean.

Remedy 3: Do not run thin ink films to produce tints. Run a thicker film of ink with lower color strength.

Remedy 4: If possible, use opaque inks rather than transparent inks.

Remedy 5: Install one or to oscillating form rollers to laterally distribute the ink.

Remedy 6: Use a GATF Mechanical Ghosting Form to determine the ghosting tendencies of the press.

Cause B:
The blanket is embossed as a result of ink-vehicle absorption during printing of the previous job.

Remedy: Install a new blanket.

NOTE: Clean an embossed blanket thoroughly with blanket wash, and hang it in a dark area. Allow the absorbed oil to diffuse through the rubber; this may reduce the embossing.

Other quality defects in web offset printing, their causes, and remedies are covered in Chapters 3–11.

Index

About GATF

The Graphic Arts Technical Foundation is a nonprofit, scientific, technical, and educational organization dedicated to the advancement of the graphic communications industries worldwide. Its mission is to serve the field as the leading resource for technical information and services through research and education.

For 73 years the Foundation has developed leading edge technologies and practices for printing. GATF's staff of researchers, educators, and technical specialists partner with nearly 2,000 corporate members in over 65 countries to help them maintain their competitive edge by increasing productivity, print quality, process control, and environmental compliance, and by implementing new techniques and technologies. Through conferences, satellite symposia, workshops, consulting, technical support, laboratory services, and publications, GATF strives to advance a global graphic communications community.

The Foundation publishes books on nearly every aspect of the field; learning modules (step-by-step instruction booklets); audiovisuals (CD-ROMs, videocassettes, slides, and audiocassettes); and research and technology reports. It also publishes *GATFWorld,* a bimonthly magazine of technical articles, industry news, and reviews of specific products.

For more detailed information on GATF products and services, please visit our website *http://www.gatf.org* or write to us at 200 Deer Run Road, Sewickley, PA 15143-2600 (phone: 412/741-6860).

Other Products of Interest from GATF

To place an order, or for more information about any of the products or services mentioned in this book, please call GATF at 412/741-6860; fax at 412/741-2311; email at info@gatf.org; or write to GATF, 200 Deer Run Road, Sewickley, PA 15143.

Products with two order numbers are available in positive (70XX) and negative (71XX) form.